QUESTAR PUBLISHERS, INC.

ESCAPING
MATERIALISM

*Living a Life That's
Rich Toward God*

GEORGE CAYWOOD

QUESTAR PUBLISHERS, INC.
Sisters, Oregon

ESCAPING MATERIALISM
© 1989 by George Caywood
Published by Questar Publishers, Inc.

Printed in the United States of America

ISBN 0-945564-12-0

Cover design: Paul Clark

Most Scripture quotations in this book are from the HOLY BIBLE, NEW INTER-
NATIONAL VERSION, © 1973, 1978, 1984 by the International Bible Society.
Used by permission of Zondervan Bible Publishers.

*In dedication to my wonderful family
through whom God has revealed so much of His love.*

*And thanks to all of you in my family and among
my friends who loved me enough to refuse to let me
quit writing this book. You read, edited, typed, cajoled,
rebuked, listened, encouraged, endured, and believed.
You know who you are — you live in California,
Oklahoma, Texas, Arizona, Virginia, and Oregon.
May God bless you.*

CONTENTS

CONTENTS

ESCAPING
MATERIALISM

INTRODUCTION

A few years ago, Pope John Paul II visited Los Angeles. Since the archdiocese offices were adjacent to Union Rescue Mission where I work, he was to be housed within a few yards of the mission's front door. The Secret Service was concerned about the possibility of an assassin disguising himself as a street person and coming to the mission in order to get close to the pope. It became necessary, therefore, for us to care for the poor at other facilities provided by the City of Los Angeles and the Roman Catholic church for that purpose. I thought well of the pope accepting to be near the poor, so I was not upset by the change in routine.

The incident aroused a great stir among the more anti-Catholic segments of the community. A few people called, angrily demanding that I denounce the pope. One man said, "Don't you know that in Latin America the Roman Catholic churches have adopted pagan religious practices into their worship service?"

"I don't know if that is true or not," I replied. "I have never been to Latin America. But are you prepared to guarantee that the pagan practices of western materialism have not crept into your church?" The man had no more to say.

Recently a book appeared in Christian bookstores denouncing the spread of eastern religious thought into our churches. It was a popular and influential book about a legitimate concern. But it brought to my mind the image of a young woman I read about in a newspaper story a few years ago. She had been kidnapped in another part of the country and finally escaped in Los Angeles, where she told the terrifying story of being raped, abused, and beaten by a couple driving around the country in an R.V. If American Christianity is in danger of being seduced by eastern religion, it was clear to me the far greater danger is that it will first be used, abused, and sold by western materialism.

Americans are anxious. Our balance of payment problem, the erosion of industry, and the waning desire of many working people to do quality work make us feel insecure. We are going deeply into debt, Christians as well as non-Christians. Few families have significant savings. We are strung out financially. Little stands between our middle-class standard of living and destitution.

When I was a boy, my mom went to work when my dad died. It was tough, but we made it. Nowadays, keeping a home usually requires that both parents stay employed. Mom is no longer in reserve; she has been placed on the front lines too. Therefore, the potential for disaster is doubled. If either mom or dad can't work, the family is in trouble.

The homeless crisis frightens us, too. Because of media coverage, the homeless now have names and faces. We are not insulated from the poor as we used to be. We are realizing that homeless people are just like us. If that ordinary person interviewed on television can end up on the street, maybe I will, too.

We hear of outrageous injustice in the world. The

people who harvest rubber make a few cents an hour. Our cars drive on their poverty. The potato chip industry throws away the most nutritious part of the potato and converts the rest to junk by soaking it in grease and salt, while millions go hungry. Racial discrimination against minority people is all too frequently entwined in the way we make daily decisions and the way we administrate the church. Some Christians cheer the cuts in government social programs, but feel no obligation to step in and fill the gap created by decimated poverty programs.

Troubled Americans are attempting to control personal anxiety by the use of drugs, promiscuity, and pleasure. We indulge ourselves in luxuries and the accumulation of things, then engage in denial so we can hide from the reality of the starving. We flip to another channel when hungry people are shown on television, and lay down magazines containing pictures of hungry children. Such avoidance blunts our personalities and dulls the enjoyment of our possessions, the very pleasure we are seeking to protect and prolong.

I Don't Want to Be a Materialist

Against each wave of anxiety and sin comes the hope of the gospel. The peace of Christ is totally unlike the peace of the world. The Spirit of God and the example of Christ stir our hearts to want to make an impact on our world.

I am struggling to understand and change. When I hear of impoverished rubber workers, I don't know what to do. I need my car to earn a living. But the fact that I feel so badly about those rubber workers is a sign that I can learn to be of help to them. God would not stir my compassion and conscience if repentance were impossible.

This book is written for other people like me, people who want to be different, but who don't know what to do about the potato chip industry or the tire industry. It is for parents like my wife and me, who want to be good parents, who struggle with the tension between the needs of our family and the needs of the hungry, between the commands of God to care for our children and the commands of God to feed the poor.

I believe it is possible to obey these directives of God. The anxiety I feel can be transformed into motivation to seek God and allow Him to teach me how to help solve the problems. Twenty years from now I would like to be powerfully addressing the economic and governmental corruption in the world. If the plight of the poor and the world's injustice to them is a problem God wants me to address, then I can depend on God to teach me to do so.

I do not want to be a materialist. I am willing to learn a different way. I want to share with you what I have learned so far.

1

LEARNING FROM A MERCIFUL FRIEND

IT WAS A VERY HOT DAY in last year's very hot summer. As I approached my driveway at the end of a long workday, the neighborhood children ran up to my car. Since we have one of the few pools in our neighborhood, the children were hoping for a swim. These children mean a great deal to me. They are wonderful people, full of energy and strength, though some of them have already had some tough breaks in life. Each child has his own means of persuasion. Some use big, hopeful eyes, some use insistent requests, others use offers to help me do the lawn or wash the car. They are charming, persuasive, and hard to resist.

That day, I yielded to them and opened the gate, giving stern instructions that no child go in the water until I changed clothes. When I returned to the pool I had decided not to swim, so was still in my business clothes. The children were lining the edge of the pool waiting for permission to jump into the water.

As I walked by the edge of the pool, I gently pushed one of the six-year-old boys into the water. He didn't seem to like it, but I was bigger and owned the pool, so he had to smile. Tommy, who had seen me push the other boy in the pool, thought it looked like great fun. I walked by him and he pushed *me* in.

As I fell into the water only one thing was on my mind: my watch. Standing on the pool floor, I held my left hand in the air to keep my watch dry, tilted my head back with my mouth out of the water and began to yell, "Tommy, this is a two-hundred-dollar watch."

Tommy was nervous. He kept saying, "George, are you mad? George, are you mad?" He was sure he had lost his right to use the pool and was upset at the prospect.

As the seconds ticked by, I saw the situation from Tommy's point of view: If it was fun for me to push his friend into the pool, it was fun for him to push me into the pool. I began to feel ashamed of myself. Now I had two problems. The first was that I had disregarded Tommy's needs and been concerned only with my watch. I had spent a good part of my day writing about escaping materialism, yet had allowed my behavior to be controlled by concern for a material possession at the expense of a child I loved. The second problem was that the watch did not cost two hundred dollars. I had lied — because, somehow, to have said "Tommy, this is a one-hundred-and-twenty-dollar watch" would not have had the impact I wanted.

The Journey to Freedom

This story graphically illustrates my point of view in this book. I do not write as someone who has arrived. Materialism has gripped me and I am in a deep struggle with it. At this point all I can do is share the insights God has given me that have allowed me to begin a journey out of materialism toward the freedom of loving God, enjoying God, and worshiping Him alone. I am hoping to join those of you who have begun the same journey and to recruit others who need to begin.

One of the primary difficulties I've had in preparing to write this book is that in studying Scripture for half an hour, I would sometimes find it necessary to then spend an hour in repentance before God. Progress has been slow. Sometimes I wept. Sometimes I was overwhelmed by anxiety because the requirements regarding wealth in Scripture were completely foreign to my experience. I asked myself repeatedly, "What am I going to do with what I am learning? How can I learn to obey what I am understanding in Scripture?" Layer after layer of materialism was being exposed in myself.

Then God gave me hope. I remembered that when I became a Christian, it dawned on me how much my life had been dominated by fear. I had been raised to be afraid. Fear had colored all my perceptions. I had been afraid of failure, afraid of people, afraid of responsibility, afraid of fatherhood. I had felt that people would reject me once they were around me long enough to realize how inadequate I was. I had suffered frequent insomnia due to the anxiety imbedded in my personality. It was the grip of those fears that had driven me to Christ in the first place.

When I first became a Christian I read John 14:1, "Do not let your hearts be troubled," and became angry. I said to God, "I don't have a button I can push or a switch I can throw to make me *not* be afraid. What do you mean, 'Don't let your heart be troubled'? You're giving me a command I can't obey. I *am* troubled. I *am* afraid. I don't know how to conquer fear." Over the next few days God helped me understand that my fears were learned fears. I

had not been born with them, but the events of my life
and the example of the people in my life as a small child
had ingrained them in me. Now, what I had learned had
to be unlearned. That process of unlearning fear and
learning to walk in truth is characteristic of my twenty-
year walk with Christ. It's been a very long process.

Now I am embarking on another long journey, the
journey away from materialism toward being in love with
God. Sometimes the journey will be difficult, often it will
be frightening, but real repentance always takes a long
time and it always hurts.

In the process of learning to live increasingly free of
fear, I have noticed a pattern. The only way God can get at
my sense of inferiority is to expose my feelings of inferiority by putting me in situations which arouse them. In the
midst of those terrifying feelings, I must put my hand in
God's hand and walk obediently through the very thing
that threatens me. If I want to learn to be joyful, I must
allow God to put me in situations that will expose those
things in me that inhibit joy. If I want to be free, I must be
willing to allow God to reveal character flaws that are
enslaving me. It is not an easy way to grow, but for those
of us deeply wounded by our own sin and the sins of
other people in our lives, it is the only way to security, joy,
and freedom.

I ask the alcoholics coming to Union Rescue Mission
for help, "How long have you been drinking?" The
response might be, "Twenty-five years." Then I ask, "For
every year you spent learning to be an alcoholic, are you
willing to commit one month unlearning alcoholic thinking?" I want them to realize that renewing their mind and
changing patterns is a long process.

Many Americans are victims of what I call "Young

Man's Disease." They think they have a choice between slow progress and fast progress. Naturally, they reject the slow progress in favor of fast progress. As we mature, life teaches us that our choice is not between slow progress and fast progress, but between slow progress and no progress. There are no quick answers. It is either a long hard road or no road at all.

I'm fifty years old now, and in regard to materialism I don't want to have Young Man's Disease. I'm not looking for quick and easy answers. I am willing to embark on a journey to lead me away from what has become a grief and a burden to me, and I'm looking for company.

God: Friend or Enemy?

This journey is such a long and difficult one that only the steady, moment-by-moment love of God can give us the courage to begin and the strength to keep going. We are to learn a new way of thinking so we will live as Christ did. The changes necessary in thinking and living are so sweeping that only God's love is a sufficient basis for success. That is why Paul spends eleven chapters of Romans to hammer home the message of God's great mercy before he invites us to renew our minds and to offer our bodies as a living sacrifice:

> Therefore, I urge you brothers, in view of God's mercy, to offer your bodies as living sacrifices, holy and pleasing to God — which is your spiritual worship. Do not conform any longer to the pattern of this world, but be transformed by the renewing of your mind. Then you will be able to test and approve what God's will is — His good, pleasing and perfect will. (Romans 12:1-2)

Only when we have established this foundation of God's mercy is it possible to lay down our lives. Paul did not say that in view of God's wrath or in view of God's justice or God's holiness we are to be living sacrifices. Our sinfulness paralyzes us if all we know of God is His holiness. But when we know God's mercy, we have the courage to face our sin boldly and to learn to live differently.

This discussion will involve the necessity of including our wealth in this process of changing our thinking based on God's mercy. I want to move away from self-indulgence to generosity. To do so, I must believe deeply in God's love. I might have an occasional burst of generosity on the basis of fear and intimidation, but only an acquaintance with God's mercy can make me, at heart, a generous person. Only God's mercy can bring me to a lifestyle of joyful giving.

If you are afraid of God, you will regard Him as an enemy. An enemy cannot teach you a thing. You can only learn from a friend. God wants you to know He is your friend and He will help you. If you do not understand that, you can have all the mercy in the world, but never begin the long journey to freedom, joy, and victory.

Not long ago, I met a man as I was going to lunch. I could tell by the intense look in his eyes that he was troubled. He wanted to talk to me. In the course of our conversation I told him, "It's important that you know Jesus loves you...just like you are."

He said, "You can only say that because you don't know what I've done."

"Well," I replied, "I know what I've done and I doubt if you're that much worse than me. I *know* God loves you."

He answered, "But you don't know what I've done."

I replied, "Why don't you tell me what you did that you think is so awful God can't love you?"

He told me he had been in the army in Vietnam and had, with his fellow soldiers, wiped out whole villages — men, pregnant women, children, grandparents. "Do you still think God loves me?" he asked.

I looked at him and felt his fear. "Your problem is your arrogance," I answered. "There is nothing in you anywhere nearly as big as God, including your sin. What you did was really very evil, but your sin is to God's love as a match is to a fire hose. My sin and yours together are no challenge at all to the mercy of God."

No More Jails

You and I *must* come to God on the basis of His mercy and friendship. If we attempt to come to Him by focusing on His demands, a strange thing occurs. We find ourselves moving further and further away from Him, doing the very things we hate. In fact, Scripture says that the righteous law of God provokes in the rebellious heart the very desire that is forbidden. Mankind is rebellious by nature. Therefore, when a command comes to us unaccompanied by God's love we rebel. It's as if we are looking for a chance to express our rebellion and the command presents the opportunity. In Romans 7 the command Paul uses to make his point is covetousness. If, in reading this book, you receive only a legalistic command not to covet, the book will serve only to arouse in you that very desire.

Only Jesus Christ can deliver us from this trap. As Paul states in Romans 7:24, "What a wretched man I am! Who will rescue me from this body of death? Thanks be to God — through Jesus Christ our Lord!"

The question is: *How* will He deliver us? The answer is in two parts. First, He removes the condemnation, or penalty of the law. Paul says, "Therefore, there is now no condemnation for those who are in Christ Jesus" (Romans 8:1). The reason this is true is because Christ died at Calvary paying the penalty for our condemnation. If we are in Christ, the penalty has been fully dealt with. The gospel is based on God's mercy. Fear and threats make us slaves to sin, but love sets us free. God's answer to sin is to remove the threat and then to richly reward us for obedience.

Remember, Paul in Romans 7:24 is not talking about people who want to sin, but about people who have the Holy Spirit within them and are, therefore, filled with a desire to be holy. You cannot have the Holy Spirit and be content in sin. The person under discussion in Romans 7:15-19 is the person who wants to do right but ends up doing wrong:

> For what I want to do I do not do but what I hate I do...I have the desire to do what is good, but I cannot carry it out...For what I do is not the good I want to do.

The wretched person is not the evil person who is succeeding in being evil, but the redeemed person who wants to do right, does not succeed, and is miserable about it. The evil person has no right to read God's answer in Romans 8. The wretched person must read it, understand it and live by it if Jesus is to deliver him. The redeemed but miserable person begins to escape the clutches of sin when he realizes Christ has absolutely removed the condemnation.

In this country, generally speaking, if you don't break the law you don't have to go to jail. But Paul is not talking in those terms. He is inviting us to live where there are no jails. For the redeemed person, condemnation doesn't exist at all. Spiritually speaking, the jails have been destroyed. This is far better than merely escaping condemnation, because now we are able to discipline ourselves not to sin. The Old Testament law had stated, *If you obey you can have peace.* But the gospel of Christ *begins* with peace. It says, *Since you have peace, obey.*

Obedience is not an option with God. It is required. But in Christ, the foundation for obedience is not self-discipline. Instead, the foundation for obedience is the incredible mercy of God that removes our fear, thereby making it possible for us to be taught a new way of thinking and responding. In other words, to embrace God's mercy is to learn to think like God. Then, because our minds are renewed, we act differently. We do not conform to wicked lifestyles, but instead receive authoritative power to live a godly life.

If we are to journey away from materialism, we must first of all embrace God's mercy until our hearts become quiet and we lose the fear of condemnation. Then, because we are not afraid, we can learn a new way of thinking about the material world. Because we think as God thinks in regard to money, we will be free to live in a non-materialistic way.

We Desire Too Little, Not Too Much

That brings us to the second part of God's answer to the question posed in Romans 7. God offers us a tremendous reward when we live in obedience through renewed minds. He makes us joint heirs with Christ, promising us a share in His glory (Romans 8:17). In other words, if we submit ourselves to His Spirit we will end up jointly owning the inheritance of Christ; and that inheritance includes the entire universe.

The appeal of the gospel is not just that God will make us pure and therefore able to resist sin so we can go to heaven, but that along with purity will come the overwhelming satisfaction of our fundamental desires. We will not covet because it is not possible to covet in a situation where you have everything anyway.

Heaven is in every sense infinitely better than earth. There is no joy on earth that will not be experienced to a higher degree in heaven. That is what makes the good news so very good. As long as we live here on earth we must live within restraints, but in heaven God will totally satisfy our deepest longings.

Christ once made the remark that in heaven there will be no giving or taking in marriage. Unfortunately, we have interpreted that to mean there will be no sexuality in heaven. This has to be a false interpretation because sexuality is rooted in the nature of God Himself. We are, after all, created in the image of God: male and female. So, to say there will be no sexuality in heaven cannot be true. Jesus was explaining that there will be no need for uniting men and women in marriage because we will already be one with each other and with God. He does not mean that in heaven we'll be so absolutely pure we won't be lustful, but that in heaven the drive for union with another person will be once and for all completely fulfilled. Human sexuality is a mere hint at the pleasure of union with God and with His universe that we will experience in heaven.

God consistently says that if we follow Him, He will purify our desires and grant them overwhelming fulfillment in heaven. It is on this basis that God calls us away from our sin. It is not the threat of the law that changes us, but the appeal of a loving Father.

Our old nature can be compared to an automobile whose engine runs on the fuel of our self-condemnation. We would like to get rid of the car, but cannot, no matter how hard we try. However, we do not have to keep it filled with gasoline. We can keep the fuel gauge on empty if we refuse to play Satan's deadly self-condemnation game.

This truth applies to money. A sense of condemnation about our possessions will force us right back into a life of materialism. If we steadfastly refuse to condemn ourselves and instead accept the mercy and grace of God, we can be led out of materialism toward the incredible, mind-boggling wealth that God offers to us in eternity. Our problem, in fact, is not that we desire too much, but that we are small-time pikers; we desire too little. We should be hungry for the riches God is offering and understand that He has made a way through Jesus Christ to fulfill and satisfy us. If this book creates feelings of self-condemnation in you, I will lock you into the sin of covetousness — and I don't want to do that. Instead I want to call you to your full inheritance in Christ.

Nothing to Be Afraid Of

Fear is the enemy of learning. I know a man who can fix anything mechanical, but has a difficult time reading books. When this man works on a car and comes to a bolt he can't loosen, he complains, "Those stupid engineers in Detroit! When are they going to design a car you can work on?" When he picks up a book, he says, "Boy! I must be stupid. I must be ignorant. I can't understand this book."

So this man works successfully on cars but rarely reads a book.

When I pick up a book and can't understand it, I say to myself, "People who don't know how to write should not try to be authors." Then I put the book down and pick up another one. When I work on a car and can't fix it, it threatens my manhood. It makes me feel inadequate. So I read books and don't fix cars. My fear of inadequacy prevents me from learning how to fix my car. Fear is the enemy of learning.

I hope you will begin to read this book by refusing the fear of condemnation. God's mercy is sufficient to carry you on this journey. If you don't believe this, you won't walk with me — and that would be something I would regret.

New patterns of thinking are not learned all at one time, but by thousands of little lessons learned in progression. Sometimes I watch my wife play the piano. Her fingers fly across the keys and music comes out. It seems impossible. I'm awed because the distance between my wife's performance and my own is so enormous. I sit down with *Teaching Little Fingers to Play,* and can barely work my way through it. The fact is, I could learn to play a little bit at a time, one lesson at a time. In ten years, my fingers also could fly gracefully across the keyboard, making music. If I began with a kind and encouraging teacher, one who believed in me, I could end up being a pianist as well.

In college, I flunked or dropped out of seven consecutive semesters. I had more units of *F* on my records than most graduates have units. I learned to fear my ability to perform academically. My fears were defeating me. Years later when I returned to college, an adviser told me I needed only about one year of credit in order to earn a bachelor's degree. She assigned me all my classes, giving me no choice in the matter. I was assigned classes with the very easiest teachers, almost guaranteeing me success. She then guided me through two more years until I earned a master's degree. Each semester became progressively more difficult until I was completing courses with the school's toughest teachers. My adviser had put me on a track that gently helped me overcome my fear of failure.

In the same way, I have learned, God will help us walk in His will throughout our lives. If we want to live free of the love of money, God will gently teach us. There is nothing to be afraid of.

2

THE BIG PICTURE

EVERYONE KNOWS HOW uncomfortable it is to live in Los Angeles because of the terrible pollution. Most of God's creation here is covered with asphalt or concrete, and what's left is masked by a layer of dirty air. Raising a family in a city like this presents a difficult theological problem. In Scripture it is assumed that God's omnipotence will be understood primarily through His creation. The extreme level of pollution in Los Angeles makes this difficult. The most natural thing is to disengage oneself from getting to know God through nature, and resort to thinking of Him in a purely spiritual way.

God does not hate material things. God loves his material creation. We may be somewhat surprised when we get to know God's attitude toward the material aspect of the universe. Influenced as we are by Greek thought, we may have been brought up to feel that only the spiritual aspects of the universe are of value. The Bible presents a very different picture.

The ancient Jews lived in a pollution-free world. There were no engines to dirty the air, no electricity to mar the

night sky with light pollution. The Israelites enjoyed a dry
climate where the air must have been crystal clear most of
the time. Many of the ancient Jews were farmers or shepherds, working with the very stuff of creation, spending a
lot of their time outdoors. This intimate contact with the
wonder of the universe fills all of Scripture.

Because of the amazing work of astronomers aided by
modern space-age science, today we have far more knowledge about the universe than biblical writers did. But
most of us lack intimate contact with nature. We have
wonderful close-up pictures of faraway planets, but we do
not know the sky as a friend.

When I was a boy I spent summers in Tucson with my
grandparents. Like most people in southern Arizona in
those days, we slept on cots outside at night because the
house was so hot. I would unfold my mattress in the back
yard, spread out a sheet, lay on half of it and pull the
other half over me, enjoying the relative coolness of the
outdoors. Night after summer night I fell asleep looking at
the beauty of the sky.

My own children have not been so fortunate. But one
night when they were small we drove up into the San
Bernadino Mountains, parked the car, and sat out on the
hood. As our eyes adjusted to the darkness, our children
had their first real contact with the stars in a clear, unpol-
luted sky. A feeling of awesome fear from the sight of the
vast number of lights nearly overwhelmed them, and they
wanted to get back inside.

Another time, when our daughters were teenagers, we
were on our way home with several of their friends from a
championship football game well away from the Los
Angeles area. I pulled off the road in a remote area. One
fifteen-year-old girl saw the Milky Way for the first time in

her life. "What is that white stripe in the sky?" she asked. I had the pleasure of explaining to her it was the galaxy we live in, our particular family of stars.

These experiences have given us brief encounters with the wonders of the sky and its revelation about the greatness of God. But to the Jews this was common, everyday experience. They grew up visiting with the stars each night of their lives.

Perhaps we can feel some of this same wonder if we take a look at modern scientific knowledge. One of the greatest devotional readings I have encountered is the May 1974 issue of *National Geographic* magazine. This issue helped me comprehend the enormity of the universe. As I read the article on outer space I thought of our family vacations. On cross-country trips we can make six hundred miles a day if we really push it. (We would have a better appreciation of just how that is if we had made the journey by wagon train a hundred years ago, traveling at one or two miles per hour.) But how long do you think it would take to drive from here to the sun if you made the trip in a car averaging six hundred miles a day? It would take you 155,000 days to drive those 93 million miles. That's almost 425 years of driving.

With that vastness in mind, consider this:

Imagine that the thickness of this page represents the distance from earth to sun. Then the distance to the nearest star is a 71-foot-high sheaf of paper. And the diameter of our own galaxy is a 310-mile stack, while the edge of the known universe is not reached until the pile of paper is 31 million miles high. (*National Geographic*, May 1974, page 592)

God So Loved the Cosmos

God's regard for material things is reflected in His decision to create so much of it. On the basis of the reality of the incomprehensible hugeness of the universe we must realize that God values the material aspects of His creation, not just the spiritual aspects.

The creation story wonderfully adds to our respect for the universe. At the end of each of the first five days of creation, God paused and reflected on what He had made. He said to Himself each evening, "It is good." And at the end of the sixth day, when creation was complete, God looked at everything He had made and said, "It is very good." When God made the material world, He was extremely pleased with it.

I can relate to that feeling of satisfaction in a limited way. I love to build things. Most of the furniture in our home I have either built or refurbished myself. I know the pleasure of being involved in a creative task and then reflecting to myself when it's finished, "It's good. I like that!"

As we evaluate the material aspects of our lives, we must consider the basic goodness of material things. God declared creation good, and our viewpoint must comply since we have been made responsible for it:

> Then God said, 'Let us make man in our image, in our likeness, and let them rule over the fish of the sea and the birds of the air, over the livestock, over all the earth, and over all the creatures that move along the ground.' (Genesis 1:26)

After God created the material world He turned it over to mankind to manage. We are to rule authoritatively over all He created. It is a good creation, full of beauty. We are designed to have dominion over it. What does this mean?

God gave Jerelyn and I four beautiful daughters: Gina, Jill, Janelle and JoAnna. When they were growing up, my God-given authority over the girls was based on my love for them, my respect for them. I was allowed to rule, not so that I could use them or abuse them, but in order to care and provide for them, to bring them to full maturity. My children were my joyous responsibility. Any abuse toward them put at risk my right to be responsible for them.

We are obligated to exercise rule over the earth in that same spirit. God admired His own handiwork and said it was good. Clearly, the creation account teaches us we have no right to abuse the world we live in. In fact, it teaches that we are responsible for its welfare.

To develop a proper attitude toward the physical universe, we need to see it in relationship to the work of Jesus Christ on earth. Look with me at the most familiar verse in the entire Bible, John 3:16: "For God so loved the world that he gave his one and only Son, that whoever believes in him shall not perish but have eternal life."

The Greek language contains adequate words that could have been chosen to refer to people or groups of people as the object of love. But when the Holy Spirit inspired John 3:16, He chose the word *cosmos* — God so loved the cosmos. This word is the root of the word *cosmetic,* and implies beauty, order, and harmony. It refers to all of God's creation. The giving of the Son of God was for the sake of the cosmos, for the sake of the beautiful things God had made, the entire universe. The gift of eternal life to you and me is a revelation of God's love for His cosmos.

The order of authority at creation was first God, then mankind, then the rest of creation, with special emphasis on the earth. David in Psalm 8:5 says it this way: "Yet Thou hast made him a little lower than God, and dost crown him with glory and majesty!" (American Standard Version). Some translations say, "a little lower than angels" or "heavenly beings." The Hebrew word used is *Elohim*, commonly translated "God" in other places in Scripture. The idea is not that we are only slightly lower than God. God is infinitely more glorious than we are. But in the order of authority we are next in line after God. You can think of it in terms of an organizational chart. God on top, then mankind reporting to God, and beneath mankind, all the rest of creation.

<u>God</u>
|
<u>Mankind</u>
|
Creation

When Adam and Eve sinned, the formula changed. God was still on top, but Satan elevated himself to the level of mankind and began to compete with him for rule over the earth:

<u>God</u>
|
<u>Mankind versus Satan</u>
|
Creation

We must never think of Satan as God's opponent. The universe is not engaged in a struggle between God and an evil power. The struggle is between *mankind* and an evil power. Satan is no challenge to God. Satan is the opponent of men and women. His sphere of influence — like that of mankind — is limited to the earth.

In 1988 I had the opportunity to see the deciding game of the NBA World Championship series between the Los Angeles Lakers and the Detroit Pistons. It was the most tremendous sporting event I ever attended. Both teams were strong and finally, to my joy, the Lakers triumphed! Suppose that these Lakers had played the seventh-grade girls basketball team at a local junior high school. The Lakers would totally and utterly defeat them. A much greater mismatch is that between God and Satan. In fact, it is no match at all. No, Satan is the opponent not of God but of mankind, and he is vying for rule over the earth.

When Christ came He reestablished the authority of mankind for those who act in His name. God is still on top, and mankind acting in the name of Jesus Christ is in a position of exercising dominion over creation, including Satan.

God

Mankind

All of creation
(including Satan and the entire universe)

The rule of mankind has now been expanded to include the full universe. God is going to give us rule over His entire universe.

There are two important results of this reestablishment of the natural order of creation. First, Satan and his demons are mentioned specifically as being subject to mankind. This was a shocking development to the disciples. With surprise and excitement they exclaimed, "Lord,

even the demons submit to us in your name" (Luke 10:17).
Jesus answered them,

> "I saw Satan fall like lightning from heaven. I have
> given you authority to trample on snakes and scorpi-
> ons, and to overcome all the power of the enemy;
> nothing will harm you. However, do not rejoice that
> the spirits submit to you, but rejoice that your names
> are written in heaven." (Luke 10:18-20)

Jesus saw that Satan could be kicked out of the heavenly realm and returned to earth, because now the disciples were equipped to deal with him. To Jesus, the joy did
not lie in the fact that mankind once again had authority
over Satan. To say they had authority over demons was
only to say that things were now back to normal. God had
always intended for men and women to rule over His
entire creation. We were intended to be children of God, to
rule with Christ. But when Satan elevated himself to the
level of mankind, God responded by becoming a man and
pulling humanity up to union with Himself. The true
wonder was that the disciples were now in a position to
participate in *heavenly* things.

Ruling the Galaxies

The second result of the re-establishment of creation is
that we become co-heirs with Christ, God's Son. We are to
inherit with Him the entire universe:

> Now if we are children, then we are heirs — heirs of
> God and co-heirs with Christ, if indeed we share in his
> sufferings in order that we may also share in his glory.

I consider that our present sufferings are not worth comparing with the glory that will be revealed in us. The creation waits in eager expectation for the sons of God to be revealed. (Romans 8:17-19)

Imagine this with me: If there is something like one hundred million galaxies in the universe, each consisting of one hundred to four hundred billion stars, and if, since the beginning of the world, there have been two billion people saved by the grace of God (nobody can know the exact number, of course), then on the average each Christian, as a co-heir with Christ, is going to end up ruling fifty galaxies full of stars!

Now we can fully understand the meaning of John 3:16. God loved what He had made — the cosmos — so much that He gave Jesus so that mankind would be restored to the position of authority. When humanity is restored to the full position of rule over creation, order and beauty will result and the fulfillment of creation will be achieved.

The issue at stake is more than the salvation of human beings from sin. Personal salvation is a priceless gift, to be sure. But the issue is the restoration of the order and purpose for creation. In Christ the original plan of God is re-established and put back on track, providing a complete picture of why God sent Jesus Christ.

God had enough respect and love for the material to create a vast universe of it. Afterward He looked upon it and said, "It is very good." Then He made mankind responsible for His creation. When earth was corrupted by sin, God sent Jesus Christ to die so that mankind might be saved *and* restored to rule.

As we look to the future of the material world, we see

some wonderful things. In the book of Revelation the walls of heaven are described as being made of jewels, the streets as being made of pure gold. When I meditate on the great pictures of the heavenly city given in Scripture, the Hearst Castle in San Simeon, California, home of William Randolph Hearst, becomes a garden tool shed by comparison. No human being, however rich, has ever enjoyed opulence to the level described in the book of Revelation.

This may be one reason why the apostle Paul in Ephesians 3:20 exclaims, "Now to him who is able to do immeasurably more than all we ask or imagine, according to his power that is at work within us...!" Our most vivid imaginary picture of what we are going to experience in terms of wealth and glory falls short. We must understand what our eternal destiny entails. In *The Weight of Glory*, C. S. Lewis put it this way:

> It may be possible for each to think too much of his own potential glory hereafter; it is hardly possible for him to think too often or too deeply about that of his neighbor. The load, or weight, or burden of my neighbor's glory should be laid daily on my back, a load so heavy that only humility can carry it, and the backs of the proud will be broken. It is a serious thing to live in a society of possible gods and goddesses, to remember that the dullest and most uninteresting person you talk to may one day be a creature which, if you saw it now, you would be tempted to worship, or else a horror and a corruption such as you now meet, if at all, only in a nightmare. There are no ordinary people. You have never talked to a mere mortal. Nations, cultures, arts, civilization — these are mortal, and their life is to ours

as the life of a gnat. But it is immortals whom we joke with, work with, marry, snub, and exploit — immortal horrors or everlasting splendors.

This is the backdrop against which we will be discussing the relationship between the Christian and the material world. God created a vast universe and said, "It is good." Jesus died in order to restore the universe to its full potential, achieved as redeemed people rule over it. Our future is one of incredible wealth and power! If we don't understand that, we will never correctly understand how we can escape the bondage of materialism while living in a material world.

We must not fall into Greek ways of thinking. Greek dualism teaches that the spiritual world is good and the material world is evil. We can see traces of that problem in the New Testament.

This is how you can recognize the spirit of God: Every spirit that acknowledges that Jesus Christ has come in the flesh is from God, but every spirit that does not acknowledge Jesus is not from God. This is the spirit of the antichrist... (1 John 4:2-3)

The problem John addressed was that people who believed the physical world is evil had a hard time accepting that God came as a physical man, a fleshly man. To the early Christian, the challenge was believing that Christ was fully human and had a fully human body, because Greek philosophy dominated world thought. John wanted to make clear that we must believe Jesus has come in the flesh.

Enough for Now

The physical world in and of itself is not evil. It's wonderful. It's good. We need to celebrate the material world. We need to enjoy the material world. We need to learn from the material world because we will ultimately rule over it. But we serve only God.

We have seen the wonderful story of what happened before the Fall of mankind, teaching us about the creation of the material universe. And we know that after the second coming of Christ we will, according to God's incredible promise, enjoy joint rule over the universe. How, then, are we to relate to the material world between the Fall and the Second Coming?

Jesus is going to make us incredibly wealthy in eternity, but for the sake of redemption we must be willing to lay it all down as long as we are living in mortal bodies in this world. Jesus taught us not to use material resources for our own selfish purposes. We are to use them for the kingdom of God. Jesus taught us to resist laying up treasures in this world, and to prepare for the next world by using our resources to reach people who still haven't heard how God loves them. God is saying to us, *Be content if you have food and clothing; in this world, in this situation, that is enough.*

That is why we are forbidden to covet. To covet is to set ourselves in opposition to God. In the next world we won't have to worry about being covetous. This is true not so much because we will be perfect, but because in the next world all our desire will be satisfied already. What will there be to covet if we are ruling fifty or sixty galaxies? We will be wealthy beyond our current capacity even to dream.

Our love for the material is not evil in and of itself. We are capable of loving the material world because we are created in the image of the God who loves the material world. The biblical command "Do not love the world or anything in the world" (1 John 2:15) refers to the political, economic, and social power systems, not to God's creation.

We have seen in the creation story and in God's giving His Son to save the world that we must share God's love for creation. It is a love that will be fulfilled absolutely in heaven. Christ temporarily abandoned His godly riches and became poor for our sake. Now Christ has been highly exalted by God. Christ calls us to live by the same standard. All we have, all we are, must be committed to the war we are waging to bring God's love to the world. Any sacrifice we make will be enormously rewarded when we enter the next age.

Burned

The redemption of man is always one step ahead of the renewal of the rest of creation. In the age before Christ, neither man nor creation was renewed because Christ had not yet died. In the present age man's renewal has begun, but the rest of creation remains in a state of decay. In the coming age, the millennial age, man will be fully, physically redeemed, and the redemption of creation will begin. Man will be trained to be the kind of leader God designed him to be. At the end of the millennial age, the earth will be destroyed by fire, then re-created unscathed by sin and given to a people fully prepared to have dominion over it and to bring honor and glory to God.

Years ago our kitchen stove broke. Someone gave me

another stove that had been sitting outdoors for a long time but was still in working condition. I brought it home and took a hose, soap, and strong cleansers to it. It seemed to work well, and my wife was grateful.

A few days after I installed it there was a scream from the kitchen. I came running to see what had happened. After Jerelyn had lit the oven, cockroaches had started running in every direction, up the kitchen walls and across the floor. It was the beginning of a major cockroach problem in our house. We took everything out of the cupboards, washed and sprayed them, and put it all back in. Everything would be fine for a couple of weeks, then the cockroaches would reappear. We repeated the process again and again.

Then I read in an article called "Indomitable Cockroach" that the weakness in the creature is a waxy coating that keeps its body fluids from evaporating. If that waxy coating is destroyed, the cockroach will die in just a few hours as its fluids evaporate. The article stated that common boric acid will destroy that waxy coating. So we bought boric acid and once more cleaned and emptied all the cupboards, putting a little boric acid in the back corner of the stove, on each shelf in the kitchen, and under the refrigerator. Within a few days the only cockroaches we saw were gathered around a dripping faucet at the sink.

In that same article a Dr. Carpenter was quoted as saying, "Other than destroying the planet, probably nothing we can do will have much effect on the cockroach." I thought about that statement in light of 2 Peter 3:10: "The heavens will disappear with a roar; the elements will be destroyed by fire, and the earth and everything in it will be laid bare." Between now and the time when all the universe will be put under our rule, the planet earth must be destroyed by fire. One of the things that fire will accomplish will be the eradication of the cockroach!

It is said of William Randolph Hearst that he spent more money on himself than anyone in history. But if he was not a follower of Christ, his regret will be that he allowed Satan to rip him off. He will look at the possessions he enjoyed on earth, compare them to the wealth of the humblest saint of heaven, and say, *I gave up this wealth for what I had on earth? I am a fool, I am a bad investor, I've been burned.*

Several years ago in New York City, the owner of an exclusive apartment full of priceless furnishings purchased some big canvases and cheap paint. He rolled colors onto the canvasses and hung them on his wall. Then he put price tags in the corner of each canvas: "$200,000." When thieves broke in, they took the valueless paintings and left his expensive jewelry, electronic equipment, silverware, and furniture.

We operate at the level of these thieves when we become enamored of the wealth of this world in a way that cheats us of the riches God offers in eternity, riches that will make the wealth of this world seem sickly in comparison.

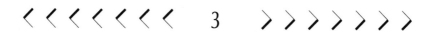

3

THE LOVE
GOD HATES

ABOUT A YEAR AGO in my devotions I was reading the
tenth chapter of Luke's Gospel where Jesus is challenged
by an expert on the law. Jesus asked the man to summa-
rize the law and the religious lawyer said, " 'Love the
Lord your God with all your heart and with all your soul
and with all your strength and with all your mind,' and,
'Love your neighbor as yourself.' "

Jesus replied, "You have answered correctly."

I began to pray and to seek the Lord. I said, "Lord, I
know Your nature. You would never give a command that
is impossible to obey. I will take this command from You
as one I can learn to live by. I believe it is possible for me
to love You in this life with all my heart, all my soul, all
my strength, and all my mind."

I confessed, "But Lord, this simply is not true in my
life now. If I loved You with that kind of love, things
would be really different for me. I'd be much happier.
God, I want You to teach me to love You with this total
love and to love my neighbor as myself."

As I meditated on this passage, I felt deeply that with

this penetrating command would come a penetrating
mercy to make obedience possible. I thought of the scriptural teaching "We love because he first loved us" (1 John
4:19). The happy result, obviously, would be that before I
could love God totally I was going to realize how totally I
was loved by Him.

At this point I was in the middle of my study for this
book. I had become aware of my love of money, aware
that this love of money was keeping me from knowing
God's love. If I continued to trust in money for security I
could never know God as my Abba Father.

Money Is a Liar

I have always been afraid of not being able to save money.
I have always been afraid I would not be able to support
my family. These fears were deeply ingrained in me
because my father was not able to support my mother and
me. In my childhood home we went hungry at times. I
grew up with the fear of going to bed hungry. As an adult,
I based my security on the size of my paycheck.

In California, a craziness occurs from time to time as
the state lottery begins to escalate in value. If someone
doesn't win for a while the prize escalates to the range of
twenty-five or thirty million dollars. When that happens,
people frantically spend their money on lottery tickets.
This pushes the prize into the fifty- or sixty-million-dollar
range. People join the mania because they believe intense-
ly that money will bring deliverance from struggle and
problems, from the daily grind, the sweat of the brow, the
labor necessary to make it in this world.

Jesus warned of the "deceitfulness of riches." The best
riches can do for us is match our emptiness. Riches can

never meet our need. Only God can do that. Only God is an adequate foundation for life. Money makes promises to us that only God can keep. Money is a liar.

Paul lived a life filled with struggle. But he also wrote,

> For our light and momentary troubles are achieving for us an eternal glory that far outweighs them all. So we fix our eyes not on what is seen, but on what is unseen. For what is seen is temporary, but what is unseen is eternal. (2 Corinthians 4:17)

Paul dismisses his troubles as light and momentary, though by his own testimony he said earlier, "We do not want you to be uninformed, brothers, about the hardships we suffered in the province of Asia. We were under great pressure, far beyond our ability to endure, so that we despaired even of life" (2 Corinthians 1:8). Paul based the ability to endure severe trials on his eternal values. The trials he encountered, though painful, were dealt with in context to his trust in God's ability to help him on earth and reward him in eternity. Paul had learned that in crisis, the only reliable source is God, Himself.

If you build upon temporary, unreliable sources you will continue to experience distress and to have a sense that life is dangerous. You will be constantly aware of your own personal inadequacy. But if you build an eternal foundation you will experience true security. God says, *Don't waste your resources on the lottery; run to my everlasting arms and I will make you truly secure.* Money is vulnerable to inflation, theft, embezzlement, and devaluation. God is invulnerable. Clearly, God is the better place to invest.

God wants to make us secure and to give us joy. When

we turn from Him, we lose our chance at the real thing. If we allow money to become our task master because it promises safety and happiness, we will turn inward and be miserable. If we serve God, even in the midst of great adversity and severe trial, we will be safe and experience overflowing joy, because our security is based on His omnipotence.

We must seek to complete our understanding of God's omnipotence. Since the creation story is the foundation for the rest of Scripture, it is the place to start. To develop our discussion it is helpful to have an understanding of ancient poetry.

English poetry tends to be built on rhythm and the repetition of sounds, especially rhymes. When a poem depends so much on sound, much of its poetic richness is lost when it is translated into another language.

In ancient Hebrew poetry, the poetic richness comes much less from the sound of words, and more from the meaning of words. As an element of rhythm, the writers of Old Testament poetry often used parallelism — the meaning of one line paralleled (was either the same as or just the opposite to) the meaning of another corresponding line. Therefore, biblical poetry translates into other languages beautifully.

Similarly, Old Testament poets created emphasis by repetition — for example, repeating a word or concept three times to emphasize it, as in Isaiah 6 where God is described as "Holy, holy, holy." In English we would typically use superlatives and say, "God is incredibly, amazingly holy."

This repetition for emphasis can also be seen in the creation poem. Creation is described in three pairs of days:

Day 1— Light	Day 4— Sun, moon, stars, seasons
Day 2— Oceans and sky	Day 5— Sky animals, sea animals
Day 3— Dry land and land plants	Day 6— Land animals, and man

Compare day one with day four, day two with day five, and day three with day six. The construction of the creation story is poetic. This is not to say the account is not literally true. It is both true and a poem. I think it is tragic that our debate with science over evolution has caused us to dissect and analyze the first chapter of Genesis as if it were some sort of lab animal. Truth is expressed in poems so that ideas can penetrate us deeply. It seems to me that poetry allows us to express our most profound thoughts in the shortest form. I occasionally write a poem when I need to say something with power and economy.

The first chapter of Genesis is a powerful poem. All of creation is summed up beautifully in just thirty-one verses. Think back to our previous discussion of the enormous size of the universe. Now think about the minuscule details God created. Scientists tell us that the smallest particles in creation are smaller than man by the same proportion that man is smaller than the universe. This diverse and complicated creative act is reduced in its purest essence to just one chapter in the Bible.

When I read the first chapter of Genesis as a poem, I understand the important difference between God and His creation. God speaks into chaos and order is the result. One moment nothing but God exists. Then God speaks and a complex universe exists. God is above, altogether different from, and separate from creation. If Gene-sis 1 really penetrates your mind, you understand that worshiping anyone or anything else is transparently ludi-crous, the ultimate foolishness.

The creation poem is an anthem that builds to its climax like Handel's *Hallelujah Chorus*. Man is the climax, the final concluding act of all creation. Man stands below God, but above all the rest of creation. Not only is it ridiculous for man to fail to worship God, but turning away from God to worship something below man, like money, is totally unthinkable.

The Worst Sin

If you do not see the difference between the Creator and creation, you cannot understand the gospel. The wonder of the gospel is that the Creator crossed the gap and lived as a creature. This fact is not shocking enough to us. Not only did God reach across the gap to us when Christ became man, but God brought us back across the gap to participate in His divine nature. He is to be worshiped for His creative power and for the incomprehensible love that makes us His children. Listen to the apostle John: "How great is the love the Father has lavished on us, that we should be called children of God! And that is what we are!" (1 John 3:1). When I read that verse I read it as if John is whispering it, overwhelmed by the implications.

The first chapter of Genesis forms the backdrop for the first chapter of Paul's letter to the Romans. If I asked you, "What is the worst sin named in Romans 1?" you might have a hard time deciding from among greed, depravity, envy, murder, strife, deceit, malice, gossip. Yet none of these qualify. These are the *consequences* of sin. The fundamental sin of mankind is that he turns away from God. God's response to sin is to abandon man to himself. The result is the kind of depravity named in Romans 1. Those things are sinful, but they are not the sin that horrifies God. The worst sin is worshiping the created rather than the Creator.

Summarizing Paul's logic we see:

A. Man turns away from God. That is sin.
B. God responds by turning man over to himself.
C. Man, as a result, destroys himself.

This basic three-step (A-B-C) logic is repeated three times by Paul in Romans 1:

A. "Although they claimed to be wise, they became fools and exchanged the glory of the immortal God for images made to look like mortal man and birds and animals and reptiles..."

B. "Therefore God gave them over..."

C. "...to sexual impurity for the degrading of their bodies with one another."

(1:22-24)

A. "They exchanged the truth of God for a lie, and worshiped and served created things rather than the Creator — who is forever praised..."

B. "Because of this, God gave them over to shameful lusts..."

C. "Even their women exchanged natural relations for

unnatural ones. In the same way the men also
abandoned natural relations with women and were
inflamed with lust for one another. Men committed
indecent acts with other men, and received in
themselves the due penalty for their perversion."

(1:25-27)

A. "Furthermore, since they did not think it worthwhile to retain the knowledge of God..."

B. "...he gave them over to a depraved mind..."

C. "...to do what ought not to be done. They have
become filled with every kind of wickedness, evil,
greed, and depravity. They are full of envy, murder,
strife, deceit and malice. They are gossips, slander-
ers, God-haters, insolent, arrogant and boastful;
they invent ways of doing evil; they disobey their
parents; they are senseless, faithless, heartless,
ruthless. Although they know God's righteous
decree that those who do such things deserve
death, they not only continue to do these very
things but also approve of those who practice
them."

(1:28-32)

Since Paul is making a fundamental point here, he
repeats it three times. The beginning of all trouble occurs
when we turn away from the Creator to worship the created. We tend to think that unsafe streets, sensuality,
drunkenness and the like are national sins that ought to be
addressed with our greatest concern. However, the real

problem in our country is that we have turned aside from the Father God. He has responded by beginning to turn us over to the desires of our own hearts. Predictably, the disaster is painful and threatening.

In *The Great Divorce*, C. S. Lewis remarked, "There are only two kinds of people; those who say to God, 'Thy will be done,' and those to whom God says, in the end, 'Thy will be done.'" God has begun to say to our nation, *Since you seem to want to live without me, I am going to let you have your way.*

Once I was talking to the son of a famous movie star. He was a homosexual. I read him the passage of Scripture in Romans 1 and asked, "Does that remind you of anything?"

"Yes," he answered. "It sounds like Hollywood."

God's judgment on America is that we cannot walk in our city streets safely. God's judgment on America is that we have become haters of our own children, aborting and abusing them in record numbers. These things are part of His judgment. The rapid deterioration of society is occurring because we have sinned by refusing to acknowledge the Creator. We have turned away from Him to worship money, to worship ourselves, and to worship pleasure. To be turned over by God to one's own desires is the beginning of hell.

Eternal life begins here on earth. If our eternal destiny is heaven, heaven has a way of reaching backwards into our lives and bringing us joy. If our eternal destiny is hell, hell has a way of reaching backwards into our lives, bringing us misery. The fact that our eternal destiny touches our mortal life is an act of grace on God's part. When heaven comes into our earthly lives it is a comfort to us. When we are touched by hell it is a warning to us. The anxiety and fear in America and on skid row has the smell of hell. It is a warning sign: Beware; you're not going to like what's at the end of this road; get on a different road.

Jesus Plus Nothing

If God is the foundation of the soul, there will be solid evidence in the quality of one's life. Think of life as a triangle. If God is the foundation, then it is stable. Pleasures can be enjoyed, and tribulations can be made to work on our behalf. But if we start to base our lives on anything other than God, our lives are pitched onto the point of the triangle. They will be unstable and frightening. The smallest problem might topple us. Joy will be muted when things go right because we sense that good will not last. When things go wrong we will turn to artificial comforts to camouflage the pain.

When our triangle is solid we are enriched by the physical, relational, financial, emotional, material, educational, intellectual and social gifts that may come our way. But take any one of those gifts and make it the foundation of a life, and it will be immediately transformed into a painful, life-sapping, destructive curse.

As long as God is the base we can receive His gifts as blessings in this life. In the next life the gifts He gives will be expanded beyond our wildest dreams. Physically we will be beautiful, healthy, and eternal, unlimited by time and space. Materially we will be wealthy beyond comprehension. We will be in perfect relationship with everyone and everything. All our desires will be satisfied; therefore sin will be impossible. This is the result of worshiping God and God alone.

Paul said, "May I never boast except in the cross of our

Lord Jesus Christ, through which the world has been crucified to me, and I to the world" (Galatians 6:14). If I boast
in the love of God expressed at Calvary then the world
and its pressure on me to focus on the material have no
impact. I hear people, including Christians, boast about
many things. One boasts of athletic ability, another of
sexual prowess, another of education. Part of the power of
money is that if we lack athletic skills, we can buy season
tickets to the Lakers and ride on their feats. Money provides the opportunity to achieve position, to buy academ-
ic degrees, and to sit on the board of a university. If we
choose to boast in something other than the cross of
Christ, money makes it all seem so possible.

A friend of mine took a trip to China with some members of his congregation. He ended up in a good-sized city
where he arranged to attend an underground church.
Before the service began he talked to the leading brothers.
"What are you teaching these days?" he asked. They said,
"A study of Acts." My friend got excited and said, "You
know, I just finished a study of Acts in my church, could I
share in today's service?" The leading brothers looked at
him for a moment and replied, "Well, sure, if you want
to."

So my friend preached at the service using a translator.
When he was finished he sat down and then started to
worry. After the service he went to one of the brothers and
asked, "Have I gotten you in trouble? You let a foreigner
preach." They were quick to answer, "No, but we thought
you understood. We're not in trouble, but *you* might go to
prison."

My friend was stunned. When he recovered he asked,
"Go to prison?" They replied, "Oh yes, we go to prison
four or five months of the year. But it doesn't matter. Jesus

is with us when we are not in prison. Jesus is with us when we are in prison. We are just as happy in prison as out. Life just goes on. We serve God."

When my friend related this experience to me he said, "You know, George, they live in a different world. A few Sundays before, the police had come to the service, standing in the back as a group. One of the brothers went to them and said, 'We love you. We know what your responsibility is and we want to encourage you to do what you have to do. Protect yourselves. But we're going to preach the gospel.' "

That kind of lifestyle is totally foreign to us. These Chinese leaders are showing us that it is practical to live this way even in the twentieth century. For them, all of life boils down to living for Christ. Their formula is: Jesus + nothing = Joy. That is a universal formula. If we replace the "nothing" in the formula with a material possession or a job or a bank account we are attempting to serve God and money. If we've learned that Jesus alone will make us happy, we can enjoy wealth when we have it and yet not live in fear when we do not have it. Whatever we put after the plus sign in that formula is what Satan will use to manipulate us.

Substitute God

As I write these words, I am again conscious of how very much I need to learn. I am aware that full repentance will take time. I feel very dependent on money for security. I am learning, though. I am not nearly as afraid of being unemployed as I used to be. Some months back I went to a member of the board of directors at the mission and told him, "This board is not my source. God is my source. And if you decide not to be used by Him to help support my family, then I will just walk away. God will supply. And if He chooses to let me starve to death, that just introduces me to heaven."

I do not mean to imply that the mission board is not loyal to me. They are very loyal and supportive. I must, nevertheless, for my own sake, make it clear that no human being or organization is the source of my security. I don't think I was as brave as my words sounded. I do know, however, that people can live free of the love of money in the twentieth century. I am determined to be one of them.

Let me make a few applications. First of all, no greedy person has any inheritance in the kingdom of God. "For of this you can be sure: No immoral, impure or greedy person — such a man is an idolater — has any inheritance in the kingdom of Christ and of God" (Ephesians 5:5). We're going to have to swallow that. The love of money is a threat to salvation.

It is the presence of the Holy Spirit in us that makes us Christians. He is the *Holy* Spirit. His presence creates a desire to be holy. Most Christians are deeply distressed about sin in their lives. If God would provide some miracle formula to put an end to sin we would take it immediately. In fact, in the early days of my walk with Christ I begged God to take over my will so I would not sin. Of course, He never did.

If, on the other hand, you claim to be a born-again Christian but feel no obligation to submit your money to the will of God and are content to live in the love of money, I believe there is cause for legitimate concern about your relationship to Christ. I'd encourage you to go back to the cross and begin once again. If the Spirit of God resided within you, He would rival and war against your love of money because the Lord is a jealous God. He would not allow an idol to reside in your heart. If you claim to be a Christian but are living a purely materialistic life with no spiritual tension, then I question if you have really come to the kingdom at all. The love of money will threaten your inheritance in the kingdom and prevent you from being saved.

The security and peace of mind we think would be ours if we won the state lottery can only be present if we love God with all our hearts. The difficulty with money is that it is an effective and powerful idol. That is why our need to repent over the love of it is so dominant in Scripture. The Lord does not want us to be allured by a substitute god.

When my kids were infants we had a little wind-up swing that kept the baby rocking for ten minutes or so. My wife's folks came by one day. I pointed to the swing. and said, "Mom, how do you like our mechanical grandma?" After that the swing never got used when she was around. She delighted in and valued her role as the real Grandma. She did not like the idea of a substitute.

The Lord wants to be a nurturing Father God. He values that relationship with us. Now that my children are adults and have moved from home, I miss them. When they seek me out it means the world to me. Jill called late one night to share a heartache with me. The thought of her wanting to have me listen to her, though I was so far removed from the situation, is still tender. But the heavenly Father's children turn by the millions to money as if financial security and material goods could fill their need for relationship. His children rest in the lap of a substitute, deluded into thinking they are experiencing real comfort and peace, while God's plan is to provide those things for us Himself. He longs to do so.

Serving God Will Cost You

Another reason God hates the love of money is because it blunts the efforts of the body of Christ to reach out to the broken and needy of the world. To honor God and do His will in any society will require that Christians pay the lion's share of the cost. In 2 Chronicles 3 we read about the expensive temple Solomon built to the Lord in Jerusalem. And Exodus 25-39 tells about the costly Tabernacle built in the wilderness centuries earlier. My point is not to justify expensive worship structures, but to illustrate that serving God will cost you something.

> The Lord said to Moses, "Tell the Israelites to bring me an offering. You are to receive the offering for me from each man whose heart prompts him to give. These are the offerings you are to receive from them: gold, silver, and bronze; blue, purple and scarlet yarn and fine linen; goat hair; ram skins dyed red and hides of sea cows; acacia wood; olive oil for the light; spices for the anointing oil and for the fragrant incense; and onyx stones and other gems to be mounted on the ephod and breastpiece." (Exodus 25:1-7)

The Israelites were to bring personal offerings of the finest quality materials to outfit the Tabernacle in the wilderness, their place of worship. The interior of Solomon's temple in Jerusalem was entirely paneled with sexpensive wood, overlaid with gold. The Most Holy Place was incredibly opulent. No expense was spared.

Christ abandoned the riches of heaven to bring God's love to the world. The early church helped pay the apostle Paul's traveling expenses to spread the gospel to the Gentiles. Bringing God's love to the Los Angeles skid row through Union Rescue Mission costs people hard-earned cash. If Christians refuse to give generously to the work of God they are acting to separate God from people He loves. Satan has many cruel and vicious strongholds in the economic and political systems of our world, and his strongholds can never be destroyed by those whose lives are built on the love of money.

The Ten Commandments begin with those designed to purify our relationship with God: Do not have other gods; do not make idols; do not carelessly use God's name. God's first concern is our relationship with Himself. The remaining seven commandments are designed to teach us how to live in harmony with others and the creation. There is logic in this organization: First, establish your relationship with the Creator so He alone is worshiped as God; then you are in a position to deal with the other seven issues.

If a person's life is characterized by failure to be obedient in an area covered by commandments four through ten, it behooves him to check out his compliance with commandments one through three. If he consistently loses the battle against lust or covetousness, that is sufficient evidence that he has a problem in his relationship to God.

Jesus said, "You cannot serve both God and Money" (Matthew 6:24). He did not say it's *hard* to serve God and money, or it's *tricky* to serve God and money, or it's *exhausting* to serve God and money. He said, "You *cannot* serve both God and Money." It's interesting He didn't say

you cannot serve God and sex, or God and personal ambi-
tion. Those things are true too, but when He summarized
the tension inside people, He chose money as the fundamental opposition to God. If you love money you are not
in obedience to the first three commandments — and you
have little hope of obeying the others.

4

THE GREATNESS OF GOD

THE MINISTRY OF ISAIAH the prophet flowed out of an incredible encounter with God in the temple, recorded for us in Isaiah 6. In this encounter Isaiah received cleansing from guilt and a calling from God. "Then I heard the voice of the Lord saying, 'Whom shall I send? And who will go for us?' And I said, 'Here am I. Send me!' " (6:8). God agreed to send Isaiah and gave him a message and a task no minister would envy:

> He said, "Go and tell this people:
>   'Be ever hearing, but never understanding;
>   be ever seeing, but never perceiving.'
> Make the heart of this people calloused;
>   make their ears dull
>   and close their eyes.
> Otherwise they might see with their eyes,
>   hear with their ears,
>   understand with their hearts,
> and turn and be healed."
>
> (6:9-10)

I can imagine how I would have felt if God had said to me, *Go to skid row in Los Angeles. I want you to preach. And I will use your preaching to close and lock the hearts of the people on skid row.* I think I would have asked the question Isaiah asked: *How long, O Lord? How long do I have to preach that kind of message?*

And he answered:
"Until the cities lie ruined
    and without inhabitant,
until the houses are left deserted
    and the fields ruined and ravaged,
until the LORD has sent everyone far away
    and the land is utterly forsaken."

(6:11)

In other words, Isaiah was to preach until God had completed His judgment on the people. This is the attitude reflected in our discussion of Romans 1: At some point God turns people over to themselves. God had been rejected by Israel so many times He turned them over to the consequences of their refusal to worship Him.

Isaiah began to preach. At one point his message changed to a message of comfort. His original message served to harden the people's heart until judgment was complete. When God proclaimed that judgment was complete Isaiah received a new call. This time he was to preach a message of comfort and hope. But not like those of the false prophets, preaching that Jerusalem would never be conquered, that God would never allow the city or His temple to be destroyed. *Don't worry,* they lied, *your worst fears will never come to pass.*

Isaiah's comfort was a strange comfort: *Yes, the destroying nation will come,* he preached. In fact, the destroyer was to come under orders from God and empowered by God. Despite that awful prospect, the people were to be comforted and hopeful because God had chosen to be in their midst. Through suffering they would find God, be purified by God, and be used by God.

Of course, not many wanted to listen to Isaiah's preaching. The nation preferred to listen to messages based on the desires of their fearful hearts. They wanted to believe nothing bad would ever happen. Of course, bad things did happen. Then the nation turned to idols with a vengeance. Idol makers became rich as the people searched desperately for security.

A small percentage of the people lived in reality and refused to bow to idols. They found a peace based on God's nearness that allowed them to live above even the worst circumstances. They had listened to and applied Isaiah's powerful preaching about God's greatness.

So Powerful, So Tender

Now, as then, there are no promises that bad things will never happen to us. Our hope is built on God's greatness, His power, and His love. God's love can help us make sense out of the worst situation. "And we know that in all things God works for the good of those who love him" (Romans 8:28). Not all things *are* good. Some things are quite evil. But God is powerful enough, wise enough, near enough to make any situation, no matter how evil, work for the good of those who love Him.

God is not offering cheap advice. He is not a commander issuing orders dozens of miles away from the front lines. He lives by the same rules He gave us. He took the desperately evil murder of His Son and used it to bring the ultimate good: salvation for you and me and the cosmos. However, if we wish to take advantage of God's offer to work for our good, we must love Him alone and never tolerate idols.

Isaiah preached powerfully about God's greatness and goodness. There is no wishful thinking, no denial in his preaching. He faced head-on the reality of suffering. Having done so, he presented a doctrine of God that transcends circumstances anytime, anywhere.

Isaiah compares the preparation necessary for the coming of a king to the preparation necessary for the coming of God.

> A voice of one calling:
> "In the desert prepare
>   the way for the LORD;
> make straight in the wilderness
>   a highway for our God.
> Every valley shall be raised up,
>   every mountain and hill made low;
> the rough ground shall become level,
>   the rugged places a plain.
> And the glory of the LORD will be revealed,
>   and all mankind together will see it.
>   For the mouth of the LORD has spoken."
>
> (40:3-5)

In ancient days the king traveled by chariot, usually drawn by a horse. There were no shock absorbers or springs. In order to make the ride as smooth as possible, an army of slaves went ahead removing rocks in the road and filling in ruts. When the king drove through, the road was as smooth as possible. Isaiah is preaching that our King is so glorious, if you want to prepare His way you're

going to have to tear down every mountain and fill up
every valley, because only the entire earth will be an adequate highway for Him. A small eight- or ten-foot path
through the desert would do for a human king, but the
God of Israel, Yahweh God, is so awesome and glorious
that to prepare the earth for His coming you will have to
make the whole surface smooth as a marble.

Isaiah goes on to discuss the eternal nature of the
Word of God. He uses incredibly powerful imagery to
help us understand the nature and greatness of the God
we serve.

> "All men are like grass,
>   and all their glory is like the flowers of the field.
> The grass withers and the flowers fall,
>   because the breath of the LORD blows on them.
>   Surely the people are grass.
> The grass withers and the flowers fall,
>   but the word of our God stands forever."
>
> (40:6b-8)

Near Azusa, where I live, you can go up in the mountains in late spring and early summer and enjoy the beautiful, tender grass under the trees and in the meadows.
But you have to come at the right time; when hot weather
begins, the grass quickly becomes dry and brittle.

One of our neighbors has a particular kind of succulent plant. It blooms once a year. When the sun comes up
the next morning the flower wilts and is gone for the rest
of the year.

The people who wield power in our lives — our bosses
or employees, friends and enemies, presidents and prime
ministers, dictators and despots — are like the mountain
grass or this succulent plant. God wants us to remember

that the people we fear will be gone quickly. They are nothing compared to His greatness. Threats made against us will fall as quickly as the people fall. But the Word of God stands forever. This fact makes God a reliable friend and a formidable enemy. By comparison, man is an unreliable ally and a weak foe. Isaiah speaks of God as being both powerful and tender in giving help to His people:

> See, the Sovereign LORD comes with power,
>   and his arm rules for him.
> See, his reward is with him,
>   and his recompense accompanies him.
> He tends his flock like a shepherd:
>   He gathers the lambs in his arms
> and carries them close to his heart;
>   he gently leads those that have young.
>
> (40:10-11)

The strong arm of God, so powerful in defense, is tender toward us. Like a shepherd He gathers His young gently in His arms. I remember being in the delivery room just after Gina was born. The nurse handed her to me and let me carry her to Jerelyn in the next room. I remember holding this incredibly small human being against my chest, wanting to be sure I didn't drop her and yet not wanting to crush her. I walked with six-inch steps out of the delivery room, my heart overwhelmed with tenderness for this baby.

When Jill was born, circumstances didn't allow me to be in the delivery room. Her birth had been very quick and easy. Afterward I stood outside the glass window looking into the nursery at this wonderful little baby, awestruck with her beauty. I couldn't take my eyes off her.

Janelle was born crying and protesting. The nurses

cleaned her off and handed her to me. I said, "There, there, little girl, everything's going to be okay." She quit crying immediately. I was delighted.

At JoAnna's birth her older sisters put a huge pink flag in our front yard. The day we brought her home they lined up on the couch and we distributed the baby across their laps. One got the feet, one got the middle, and one got the head. Then after a few minutes they rotated, so that each girl got to hold all of their wonderful baby sister.

All these tender feelings, this awe and delight, is wrapped up in the heart of the majestic, mighty God. His mighty power is reduced to a gentle nudge with His young ones.

When our four daughters were all under age seven, Jerelyn was very tired. I was concerned for her with all the diapers to change and dirty dishes to do. I began to pray for a dishwasher. I said, "God, Jerelyn is really tired. It would be wonderful if You would give her a dishwasher."

Very clearly the Spirit of God said back to me, "Okay, you're it." Before long He even gave her an electric one. The compassion of the Lord for young mothers was described thousands of years ago by the prophet Isaiah, and His gentleness has never changed. The almighty God, who is still the tender God, gently leads those that are with young.

Dust and Waterdrops

Isaiah continues:

> Who has measured the waters
>   in the hollow of his hand...

(40:12)

Take a pan, fill it with water and set it on the table in front of you as you read this chapter. Reach into the pan, fill your palm with water, then dump it into another bowl. This is how God measured out the Pacific Ocean. Then take a partial palm-full of water out of your pan. That's the Atlantic Ocean. God is at the same time large enough to scoop out oceans and small enough to care for a little lamb.

> ...or with the breadth of his hand
> marked off the heavens?
>
> (40:12)

I have watched Jerelyn measure the children for clothes by using the span between her thumb and little finger. I have seen farmers measure a horse with their hands. God is so huge He can measure the space between galaxies with His hand. "I'll put a galaxy here," He says. Then He measures a hand span across the universe and says, "I'll put another galaxy here." Isaiah wants us to feel the awesome scope of our God. Why would anyone put their trust in an idol when the almighty Creator is personally available?

> Who has held the dust of the earth in a basket...
>
> (40:12)

Imagine a five-year-old filling a small basket with dirt, intending to make mud-pies. Or imagine a farmer carrying a basket of dirt from his fields to make a flower box for his wife. All the earth's soil together is but a basketful to God.

> ...or weighed the mountains on the scales...?
>
> (40:12)

When I was a boy our icebox was seldom full. As a consequence I love to go grocery shopping now, and it delights me to fill our refrigerator. I never feel discouraged about the cost of living. If I have enough money to restock the cupboards in our home, I rejoice. Think of me going to the apple bin at the supermarket and putting a bag of apples on a scale. In similar fashion God picked up a mountain, weighed it and positioned it — Mount Everest in its place. He picked up a handful of smaller mountains and put them in place. There were the French Alps. He sculpted them with His hands until their beauty and majesty pleased Him. Creating the earth and the universe did not tax God or push Him to His limits. It was an easy task.

> Who has understood the Spirit of the LORD,
> or instructed him as his counselor?
> Whom did the LORD consult to enlighten him,
> and who taught him the right way?
> Who was it that taught him knowledge
> or showed him the path of understanding?
>
> (40:13-14)

Isaiah asks, *Which of you did God ask for advice about where to hang a galaxy, or where to place a mountain, or how much water to fill in an ocean basin?* The answer is obvious. God had no need for advice. We cannot possibly have more knowledge than He does. Why then would we worship an idol like money that knows nothing at all? If trusting our own wisdom is foolish, to depend on an inanimate object is unthinkable.

> Surely the nations are like a drop in a bucket...
>
> (40:15)

Now you'll need your pan of water again. Stick your finger in the water and lift it out. On the tip of your finger there will be a water drop.Shake your finger and let the drop fall back into the pan. That was Russia. Now do it again, shake your finger and let another drop fall. That's China. The next drop is the United States, and so on. To our God, the most incredibly powerful nations in the history of the world are a mere drop in a bucket.

> ...they are regarded as dust on the scales...
>
> (40:15)

Imagine taking a rag to dust off the scale before you weigh the produce at the grocery store because you don't want to pay for the dust along with the fruit. Of course, you would never do that. Obviously the dust on the scale has no significant weight. Neither do the nations of earth in comparison to God's eternal plan.

> ...he weighs the islands as though they were fine dust.
>
> (40:15)

Imagine a sunny afternoon with the sun streaming through your window. Look closely now. Notice the individual dust particles shining in the air. Focus your concentration on a single isolated speck of dust; that's like God taking a look at Hawaii.

> Lebanon is not sufficient for altar fires,
>   nor its animals enough for burnt offerings.
>
> (40:16)

In my imagination I can see the forested panorama of the Sierra Nevada Mountains. But there is not enough wood there to make an altar great enough for God. I imagine the vast cattle herds of the southwest. All of them put together would be an insignificant offering. Why settle for a smaller god to whom a splinter makes too great a fire or a slice of beef too overpowering a sacrifice?

> Do you not know?
>> Have you not heard?
> Has it not been told you from the beginning?
>> Have you not understood since the earth was founded?
> He sits enthroned above the circle of the earth,
>> and its people are like grasshoppers.
> He stretches out the heavens like a canopy,
>> and spreads them out like a tent to live in.
>
> (40:21-22)

At Union Rescue Mission we have a constant battle against insects. Frequently a visitor will remark, "I didn't expect a rescue mission to be so clean." I always answer, "It's either us or the cockroaches!" Many of the old buildings in the neighborhood are badly infested. One day I heard a woman employee scream. She had been frightened by a big cockroach that was quickly killed. The most powerful rulers this planet has ever known are mere insects to God, presenting no threat whatsoever.

> He stretches out the heavens like a canopy,
>> and spreads them out like a tent to live in.
>
> (40:22)

My skin cannot tolerate much sun anymore, so I enjoy the beach breezes and surf from under a canopy to protect myself from the rays. But to God all the sky is a canopy. He is so huge, He needs the universe to serve as a tent.

> He brings princes to naught...

and a whirlwind sweeps them away like chaff.
                                                    (40:23-24)

Think of the autocratic rulers appearing in the newspaper headlines this year. Now grab a handful of puffed rice from your cereal cupboard. Blow on it. This is the way the power of earthly rulers is dissipated by the almighty God.

Do You Dare to Compare?

Still Isaiah preaches on, proclaiming God's questions:

"To whom will you compare me?
    Or who is my equal?" says the Holy One.
Lift your eyes and look to the heavens:
    Who created all these?
He who brings out the starry host one by one,
    and calls them each by name.
Because of his great power and mighty strength,
    not one of them is missing.
                                                    (40:25-26)

The starry host is the crowning expression of God's greatness. According to the last count I read, our galaxy contains one hundred billion stars. That number is too large to conceptualize. Let's take it down to earth by creating an illustration using Dodger Stadium. (I rooted for the Dodgers when they were still in Brooklyn and I grieved every year when the Yankees beat them. I could not believe my good fortune when they moved to Southern California.) Dodger Stadium holds a little more than fifty thousand people. If you filled it for ten games a day, how many years would it take before one hundred billion people got to see the Dodgers play?

Suppose you started filling the stadium with fans at the beginning of the Civil War. If you kept going until today there still would not be enough time to reach one hundred billion people. Suppose you started July 4, 1776, our Independence Day. No, there still would not be enough time. Suppose you began the day Columbus discovered America. No, that's not enough time either. If Columbus had been eighty years old when he discovered America (he wasn't, but if he had been) and you began the day he was born, filling and emptying Dodger Stadium ten times a day every day until now, you would finally reach one hundred billion people who were able to see the Dodgers play. That is the amazing number of stars in our galaxy alone, which is one of the smaller ones. Scientists estimate that there are nearly one hundred billion galaxies in the universe, each containing one hundred to four hundred billion stars.

It is our God who created these stars, who brings them out one by one and calls each of them by name. Once I was sitting reading in our living room. I said, "JoAnna close the door." She didn't. Again I said, "JoAnna, close the door," and she didn't move. So again I said, "JoAnna, close the door!" She didn't move. I turned to Jerelyn and said, "Why won't that child respond to me?" Jerelyn didn't even look up from her book as she said, "It's probably because her name is Janelle." But God never refers to a star by the wrong name. He is the Creator of this incredible universe. He has the intelligence and power to keep all of it in order.

God asks a fair question in Isaiah 40: *To whom will you compare Me?* In the context of our culture the question becomes, *Do you dare to compare my ability to provide for your needs with that of your bank account?* My uncle once

asked God for one hundred thousand dollars. As he
prayed about it the Spirit of God impressed on him that
He would, instead, give him what he really wanted. What
my uncle really wanted was a sense of confidence about
his financial future. Isaiah has shown us a God prepared
to nurture us as a mother and defend us as a father. Everything we could ever imagine in a god, He fulfills. Would
you rather trust the power of money or the power of this
tender, loving, near, willing, wise, strong, big, mighty, creative God?

I believe God is looking for people who are willing to
learn how to put their whole trust in Him — and who
want to begin immediately.

5

THE FUTILITY OF IDOL WORSHIP

TO WHOM, THEN, will you compare God?
What image will you compare him to?
As for an idol, a craftsman casts it,
and a goldsmith overlays it with gold
and fashions silver chains for it.
A man too poor to present such an offering
selects wood that will not rot.
He looks for a skilled craftsman
to set up an idol that will not topple.

(Isaiah 40:18-20)

The parallel thought to the might and majesty of God is the stupidity of idol worship and the damage it does. The first evidence Isaiah gives of the futility of worshiping idols is that they are made by man. A couple of years ago I made a redwood deck in our back yard. It's very basic, just a platform about eight or ten inches off the ground. The kids enjoy sun bathing on it. Can you imagine me going up to the deck and saying, *Oh deck, deliver me? Oh deck, help me get a job?* The idea of asking something I have made myself to help me is obviously very silly.

Isaiah wrote that the idol maker "nails down the idol
so it will not topple" (41:7). It is irrational to worship
something that has to be nailed down to keep it from
falling. Just imagine a little boy running through his
home. His mom says, *Billy, will you quit running by that
idol? Every time you go by it you knock it down.* She turns to
her husband: *The next time you buy an idol, dear, buy one
with nail holes. This one's just too easy to knock over. Every
time Billy runs by, it topples over.* Dad goes out and buys an
idol with little holes in the bottom so he can nail it to the
floor and keep it steady. God asks, *Would you seriously
compare Me to a man-made idol that has to be nailed to the
floor? To whom, then, will you compare Me?* The answer is,
God, You are incomparable.

Deceit and Retreat

Next Isaiah asks, *Since you know better, why do you persist
in worshiping idols?* This question is expressed in two pairs
of questions. First, "Do you not know? Have you not
heard?" (40:21). Isaiah chided the people of his nation.
Pagan idol worship is rooted in ignorance, but for the
people of God idol worship is rooted in rebellion.

The second couplet of questions is, "Has it not been
told you from the beginning? Have you not understood
since the earth was founded?" (40:21). Isaiah is saying the
entire universe is built upon the faithfulness and power of
God. From the very beginning, the stars have come out
every night, giving beauty and light. Every morning the
sun comes up so crops will grow and people can work.
Every year summer is followed by fall, fall is followed by
winter, winter is followed by spring, spring is followed by
summer. You have seen with your own eyes the miracle of

birth; you daily use a marvelously designed piece of equipment, the human hand. Everywhere you look, everything you experience speaks of the faithfulness of God operating in the universe. The voices of creation declare that God is great and God is faithful. Why do you rebel against all that you are a witness to and turn to idols? It is lunacy. You have no excuse.

Isaiah continues:

> "Bring in your idols to tell us
> > what is going to happen.
> Tell us what the former things were,
> > so that we may consider them
> > and know their final outcome.
> Or declare to us the things to come,
> > tell us what the future holds,
> > so we may know that you are gods.
> Do something, whether good or bad,
> > so that we will be dismayed and filled with fear.
> But you are less than nothing
> > and your works are utterly worthless.
> > He who chooses you is detestable."
>
> (41:22-24)

Isaiah challenges the idols: *Tell us about the future! Oh, you can't tell us about the future? Then tell us something about the past. Oh, you can't do that either? Well, do something! Don't just sit there in the corner...do something! Act! Declare yourself!*

Money is as unreliable as any idol Isaiah ever encountered. If the poor of Calcutta had what Americans living at poverty level have, they would be overjoyed. The American poor feel they would have it made if they could just obtain the standard of living of the middle class. A middle-class American thinks, *If I had one more raise, if I could earn another ten thousand dollars a year, then I would be happy. Then I would feel secure.* The wealthy upper class strive to become ever richer. The love of money is insatiable. The rich are not happy. The rich do not feel secure. Money is a faithless, deceiving idol — promising joy, peace of mind, and security, but unable to deliver.

America is the richest nation in the world. America may well be the most anxious nation in the world as well. No nation on earth should be as conscious of the futility of wealth as America. But, unfortunately, American television is exporting materialism around the world. People in desperate economic situations are having images shown to them of wealthy Americans, fueling a hopeless desire for material things. The American television situation comedy does not show the destructive power wealth wields when it becomes the focal point of a person's life. There are no weekly programs that chronicle the demise of someone like Howard Hughes or Marilyn Monroe.

There was a time when I walked away from the pursuit of holiness and began to pursue money instead. God blessed my career and for three years I received a major promotion or raise every several months. Although my level of skill was always several promotions behind the job I was trying to do, I ended up making more money than I thought I ever would make. However, it was always the next raise that was going to make me happy. *If I could get just one more raise,* I always thought, *then we would be able to pay these bills.*

The raise would come, and for two or three paydays, we would feel the exhilaration of having more money. Then our spending would catch up with our income and we would be in exactly the same position — dissatisfied. I was pursuing the retreating goal of wealth.

God's Help on God's Timetable

Why did I pursue such a worthless idol? Why had I begun to worship money? Because money was immediately available to me. If I looked to God for help, I would be required to have faith, to trust over a long period. The help of God comes on God's timetable. In Scripture, *faith* is always connected to *time*. It always involves *waiting*.

> Even the youths shall faint and be weary,
>   and the young men shall utterly fall:
> But they that wait upon the LORD
>   shall renew their strength.

(40:31, KJV)

At the heart of any temptation is a refusal to wait for God's timing. In the story of the Fall of mankind in the book of Genesis, the serpent said to Eve, "Did God really say, 'You must not eat from any tree in the garden'?" The serpent called into doubt the goodness and faithfulness of God by suggesting that Adam and Eve might starve to death if they obeyed God.

Having created some doubt toward God's goodness, The serpent suggested that if they would eat of the fruit of the tree their eyes would be open and they would be like God (Genesis 3:5). Implied in that statement is the notion that God did not want Adam and Eve to be like Himself. Quite obviously, God did want Adam and Eve to be like Himself because He created them in His image. The desire to be like God is not an evil desire. God Himself has put it within our hearts. We are told in Romans 8:29 that Christ died on the cross so we could end up being like God. "For those God foreknew he also predestined to be conformed to the likeness of his Son."

Eve's problem was that she doubted God's determination to meet her needs. She had a desire to be like God, and in time God would have fulfilled her desire if she had trusted Him. A little further in Genesis we have the account of Enoch, who did not die, but was translated into the presence of God. I believe the Enoch story is given to us to help us understand that if Adam and Eve had not sinned, they would have had their desire to be like God fully satisfied in God's way, in God's time.

Satan's argument was that they should not have to wait on God. The fruit was dangling from the tree. The fruit (for some reason I always see a red, juicy apple) was appealing. It was immediately available. To satisfy her desire to be like God, all Eve had to do was reach up, pick, and eat. So she did — only to discover the temptation could not deliver on its promise.

For many of us the forbidden fruit is money. We imagine that if only we could win the lottery, get a raise, start our own business, we would then be autonomous. We'd really be living. But our imaginations deceive us. In fact, picking the forbidden fruit is the surest way to destruction, just as it was for Adam and Eve.

We Can Afford to Wait

Isaiah's message is that God knows us and loves us. We can afford to wait on God. He will not disappoint us.

> But now, this is what the LORD says —
>   he who created you, O Jacob,

he who formed you, O Israel:
"Fear not, for I have redeemed you;
   I have called you by name; you are mine."

(43:1)

The last phrase here gives me permission to insert my name into this passage. In other words,
   This is what the Lord says to you,
      He who created you, George,
      He who formed you, Mr. Caywood:
   "Fear not..."

God knows us by name. He has the hairs of our heads numbered and says to us, *Don't be afraid.* I suggest that you read this passage and put your own name into it as I have.

The reliable help of God does not mean you will never be tested or experience suffering. Yet God says to you,

"When you pass through the waters,
   I will be with you;
and when you pass through the rivers,
   they will not sweep over you.
When you walk through the fire,
   you will not be burned;
   the flames will not set you ablaze."

(43:2)

Notice that this passage does not say *if* you pass through the waters, or *if* you walk through the fire. It says *when* you do. Clearly, then, God offers us help *when* we are tired, not help to prevent us from getting tired. Some Christians resent God because their expectations are not

fulfilled. They expect God to deliver them from trial when
God has clearly promised throughout Scripture to be with
us *in* trial. We have the example of every Bible character to
support that point of view, including Christ Himself. We
all pass through waters — deep waters — and fire. We
must never listen to sloppy theology about God shielding
us from pain. If we do, we will end up disappointed,
resentful, and mistrustful of God.

Instead of telling our idol, *You have failed me,* we get
mad at God. We must clearly hear Christ when He says,
"In this world you will have tribulation." This is not our
favorite promise. We want God to guarantee that we can
continue to indulge ourselves at the level we've become
accustomed to. We look for God to arrange the circumstances of our lives so nothing will happen that would
make us respond in fear. We don't want our jobs threatened. We don't want our investments to go bad. We don't
want our health to fail, for it threatens our ability to earn
money.

We do not have a single promise from God that those
things won't occur. In fact, we are promised those things
will occur, but God is with us. He knows us by name and
He loves us. When we pass through the waters He will be
with us. God needs people who are willing to get wet for
the sake of the Gospel, and who for the sake of redemption will go through any river God requires. God needs
Christians who, for the sake of the lost and the sake of the
poor, will walk through fire and feel the sweat break out
from the heat.

Among my dearest Christian friends is a man who is
angry at God because he did not get the promotion he felt
he ought to get. There is a woman who resents God
because she injured her thumb just when she needed it to

start a new job. When I had blood clots in my legs and was laid up, I was quick to blame God. In contrast to these responses we have this word from Isaiah: "He gives strength to the weary and increases the power of the weak" (40:29). He gives us strength, but it is not like Popeye eating spinach. We grow strong through endurance in those exhausting times of testing.

When I go to my workout at the YMCA early in the morning, the place is full of people emptying themselves of physical strength. But as I look around I see that their bodies have acquired great endurance and great power. How did they get that way? Day after day and week after week they used their muscles to the point of exhaustion. As a result their strength increased.

You see, God gives strength to the weary, but we don't like to get weary. God increases the power of the weak, but we don't like to be pushed that hard. Therefore we avoid exercise. We say, *God, give me your power,* and expect it to come as we sit in the church pew. That is not the way it happens.

To become strong you must become weary. To receive the power of God you must be extended to the point of weakness. Those who exercise faith, who step out into fearful and challenging places in obedience to God, learn of God's faithfulness and experience God's security. No other means to security and joy is given to us in Scripture.

Not only so, but we also rejoice in our sufferings, because we know that suffering produces perseverance; perseverance, character; and character, hope. And hope does not disappoint us, because God has poured out his love into our hearts by the Holy Spirit, whom he has given us. (Romans 5:3-5)

Consider it pure joy, my brothers, whenever you face
trials of many kinds, because you know that the testing of your faith develops perseverance. Perseverance
must finish its work so that you may be mature and
complete, not lacking anything. (James 1:2-4)

This road is not a road we like to travel, because it
means learning to rejoice in things from which we'd rather
run. Certain prominent theologies today support our natural desire to live a life free from pain, just like the false
prophets of Isaiah's time. But a life unencumbered by
trials is not available no matter what you do, no matter
how you pray, no matter how much faith you have. Rivers
will rise and fires will rage, all by God's design. He wants
wet, sweaty children because it is the only way we will
receive His greatest blessings.

For several years Jerelyn and I picked annual slogans
for our life together. For example: "Free for Thee in '83"
and "Joy Galore in '84" and "Come Alive in '85." When
we first prayed those prayers and set those goals we did
not understand that in order to be "Free in '83" God
would have to address those things that enslaved us. In
order for there to be "Joy Galore in '84" God had to
address the things that inhibited joy. In order to "Come
alive in '85" God had to address the things that brought
death.

As someone expressed it, God has to dredge the trash
out of the bottom of our lake. God is fully prepared — in
order to purify our lake — to muddy the waters and make
its surface ripple with turmoil. When God becomes our
God He acts in a way that exposes the worst and most
painful part of our hearts. I believe this is because God can
heal only what He reveals.

Promised Judgment, Promised Help

Again Isaiah conveys God's voice:

> "Be silent before me, you islands!
>   Let the nations renew their strength!
> Let them come forward and speak;
>   let us meet together at the place of judgment."
>
> (41:1)

Our nation is beginning to experience the judgment of God. Our land is being purchased by other nations. Disease and violence are threatening our peace of mind and the lives of our families. Our economic future is dim. Frightened, disillusioned people turn to substance abuse to escape reality. We satiate ourselves with the accumulation of material things. Christians are not immune to these things. When our nation falls, we fall with it.

In ancient times, the people of the Middle East watched as a powerful army invincibly marched across their territory. In the face of the oncoming judgment, those who didn't know God turned to idolatry. God understood that those who had not been chosen by Him would turn to idols. But He implored His own people to turn away from them.

In Isaiah 41:10, God goes on to say, "Do not fear." But this implies there is something to fear. Yet in the midst of His people's confusion and fear, He assures them, "I am with you." God has never promised us a world where we will not be easily dismayed. He is not promising us a world where nothing will make us fearful. He is, in fact, promising us the opposite. Because of sin, our nation is falling apart, and God is saying, *My left hand is beginning*

*to bring judgment, but in response to that, My people, don't be
afraid. I have chosen you. I will uphold you with My right
hand.*

When God wants to bring judgment on the world, any
nation will serve as an instrument of that judgment. He
picks a nation and says, *You judge the world. I'll delegate
that to you.* But when it comes to helping His own people,
God does not delegate that to anyone. He does it Himself.
God is saying to you and me, *Don't turn to material things
as everyone around you has. I understand people's need to do
that. But you, George Caywood — turn to Me; I want to help
you. I want to bring you deliverance.*

Sometimes we turn to idols instead of God because we
don't want to be warriors. We want to avoid conflict and
live peaceful lives. But that is not what God has called us
to. God has called us to be forceful opponents of Satan.
Isaiah 41:15-16 is a wonderful passage. It says we are not
called to be bulldozers, but to be threshing machines challenging Satan's dominion, as a field of wheat is challenged
by a combine. There are beautiful people who need to be
rescued and harvested for the kingdom. In the process of
making you a victorious warrior, God will make you an
agent of change in the lives of desperate people.

The issue, then, is this: What do you want your god to
do for you? Do you want him to make you comfortable?
Do you want him to guarantee that you can sit at ease in
your church pew? Do you want him to ease your way
through life and knock down the barriers in front of you?
Well, that kind of god is not Yahweh. If you follow
Yahweh, He will lead you through the fires. He will make
you uncomfortable, tired, and weak — in order to heal
you and make you strong and happy.

ALMIGHTY GOD OR THE ALMIGHTY DOLLAR?

IN MY DESIRE to take a fresh look at what the Bible says about money, it occurred to me that Luke — a physician who became a committed disciple of Jesus Christ — was most likely a wealthy man. If I studied his writing, I reasoned, I might gain a great deal of insight about wealth and how it relates to a Christian in a needy world.

A New King

In the first chapter of Luke's Gospel the angel speaks to Mary about the child who was to be conceived in her womb.

> "He will be great and will be called the Son of the Most High. The Lord God will give him the throne of his father David, and he will reign over the house of Jacob forever; his kingdom will never end." (1:32-33)

In royal successions from father to son, kings who come from weak fathers are disadvantaged. Kings who

come from powerful fathers begin their rule from an elevated point. Christ was conceived by the Spirit of the
Almighty and followed in the line of the greatest of all
Jewish kings, King David. Christ's rule was not to be temporary, but eternal.

The other side of the heritage of Jesus Christ is beautifully expressed in the song sung by Mary after His con-
ception. Christ has a peasant heritage through His mother,
chosen because of her humble lineage.

> "My soul praises the Lord
>   and my spirit rejoices in God my Savior,
> for he has been mindful of the humble state of his
>   servant...
> He has performed mighty deeds with his arm;
>   he has scattered those who are proud in their
>   inmost thoughts.
> He has brought down rulers from their thrones
>   but has lifted up the humble.
> He has filled the hungry with good things
>   but has sent the rich away empty."
>
> (1:47,51-53)

Mary understands here, prophetically, that in Christ is
the great reversal of all human systems. He opposes those
whom the world favors: the proud, the powerful, the rich.
The proud become scattered; those who wield power are
brought down; those who are rich end up hungry. In other
words, those who live their lives assuming their wealth
and power is a stamp of God's approval will be routed by
this King Jesus. Those whose weakness and poverty brand
them as rejects in the eyes of the world are true subjects of
this king.

The hungry people are going to be filled. I don't know what that would have meant to an Israelite living in poverty, but to me that means turkey with stuffing, enchiladas and tacos, chicken chow mein, and fresh, ripe fruit. Christ not only would fill the hungry up, but would fill them up with good things.

I have learned in my years at Union Rescue Mission that one of the most humiliating things a person can experience is a sense of powerlessness, a lack of control over his own destiny. This is true of the street people in America's cities. They have no sphere of influence or power, and are completely dependent on others to meet their needs. But with the coming of this king, the powerless will now have a representative; those who have a lifetime of humiliation behind them will be the most powerful people in the universe.

Christ's humble birth identified Him with the poor:

> And she gave birth to her firstborn, a son. She wrapped him in strips of cloth and placed him in a manger, because there was no room for them in the inn. And there were shepherds living out in the fields nearby, keeping watch over their flocks at night. An angel of the Lord appeared to them, and the glory of the Lord shone around them, and they were terrified. (2:7-9)

This baby wasn't born in a seaside chateau or a palace, but in a smelly stable. He slept in a feeding trough. His birth was announced to shepherds in a country field, not by trumpeter riding through cities on horseback the way the birth of a king was normally announced.

A shepherd in ancient society might be comparable to

our culture's parking lot attendant or dishwasher. Those
are both honorable professions by which at various times
in my life I have earned my living. I don't intend to
demean anyone who has such employment, but only to
make the point that the birth of Jesus was announced to
the shepherds because he was to be the king of ordinary
people, not of the prestigious or highly paid.

It is touching that the birth of the Christ child was first
announced by a single angel. The shepherds were not
used to being addressed by powerful beings. Once they
understood they were not being threatened, these humble
people were allowed to see the numberless host of heaven.

The angels sang this message: "Glory to God in the
highest, and on earth peace to men on whom his favor
rests" (2:14). Who are these men on whom His favor rests?
The previous prophecy of Mary had already answered
that question. The favor of God rests on the powerless of
this world, the hungry, those who are accustomed to being
humiliated. *God is worthy of praise,* the angels say, *because
the favor of God has come to men like shepherds, those who
wrestle for survival in the world, those who are humble and
those who are hungry.* The only wealthy people who were
told of Jesus' birth were a few people who were actively
seeking God, living hundreds of miles outside of the
nation of Christ's birth.

When the time came for Mary to present the sacrifice
of consecration for her new baby, she brought "a pair of
doves or two young pigeons" (2:24). According to Mosaic
law, this was the offering of a poor person:

> These are the regulations for the woman who gives
> birth to a boy or a girl. If she cannot afford a lamb, she
> is to bring two doves or two young pigeons, one for a

burnt offering and the other for a sin offering. In this way the priest will make atonement for her, and she will be clean. (Leviticus 12:7-8)

Mary soon encountered a prophet, Simeon, who had lived his entire life waiting for the coming of the Messiah. He instantly recognized that Mary's baby was the One he had been waiting for. Simeon blessed Joseph and Mary saying, "This child is destined to cause the falling and rising of many in Israel" (Luke 2:34). We need to refer back to Mary's song once again and ask, Whose falling was this child destined to cause? And whose rising was this child destined to cause? Pronounced while He was still an infant, this prophecy confirms that His effect in the world would be against the rich and the powerful while in favor of the humble and the hungry.

Where Repentance Begins

The account in Luke quickly shifts to Christ as an adult. He is now perhaps thirty years old and beginning His ministry. His cousin John was preaching a baptism of repentance for the forgiveness of sin:

"You brood of vipers! Who warned you to flee from the coming wrath? Produce fruit in keeping with repentance. And do not begin to say to yourselves, 'We have Abraham as our father.' For I tell you that out of these stones God can raise up children for Abraham. The ax is already at the root of the trees, and every tree that does not produce good fruit will be cut down and thrown into the fire." (3:7-9)

John announced that before he would baptize anyone, he wanted to see fruit in their lives, in keeping with genuine repentance. He told them not to just *say* they were repenting, but to give evidence by a changed life and behavior. The crowd was frightened. They came to John and asked a logical question: "What then should we do?"

John answered, "The man with two tunics should share with him who has none, and the one who has food should do the same" (3:11). Another group stirred by this sermon, the tax collectors, came to him and asked, "Teacher, what should we do?" His response was, "Don't collect any more than you are required to." A third group, soldiers this time, came asking, "And what should we do?" and John replied, "Don't extort money and don't accuse people falsely — be content with your pay" (3:14). The issue being addressed here was this: A soldier could threaten a common person and say, *If you do not pay me fifty dollars I'll report to my captain that you're teaching insurrection against Caesar.* A Jewish person accused of a crime would likely end up in jail. Therefore, rather than risk it, the Jew would give the soldier the money he asked for. John said to the soldiers, "Be content with your pay."

A large crowd was with John. As in any gathering of human beings, probably every kind of sin was represented there: sexual sin, hatred, involvement with evil spirits, drunkenness, and all the other familiar sins. However, when the various groups within this crowd asked John what fruit of repentance he wanted to see, the only thing he talked about was money. Share your wealth, He said: Don't collect more taxes than you ought to, don't extort money, be content with your pay. That's a powerful beginning to what Luke is teaching. In fact, I'm prepared to say that one of the primary messages of the Gospel of Luke is that all genuine repentance begins with repentance over money. The Gospel of Luke suggests that *if you haven't repented over money you haven't repented at all.*

Many years before, when the Jews had been carried off into captivity, they had finally rid themselves of the worship of statues. By the time Christ was born they might have been feeling pretty good about themselves since they were no longer idolatrous. But John tried to point out that they had exchanged one foolish idol — a statue — for the most foolish idol of all — money. They were more profoundly into idolatry than they had ever been at any time in their history.

Good News for the Poor

From the ministry of John we move on in Luke 4 to the temptations of Jesus Christ. The first temptation had to do with bread. Satan said to him, *Will God provide for You? Follow me and I will provide for You.* Of course, Jesus turned that down. So Satan upped the intensity of the temptation and said, *If You follow me I'll give You the kingdoms of this world.* This is a far greater issue than just bread for a hungry man. Satan was saying, *Abandon Your call and I will exalt You to the top of all existing political and economic systems.* Of course, this would have been in exact opposition to the role Christ was to play in the world, because He came to destroy the existing economic and political systems and to impose a new system, the kingdom of God. To give His power to existing systems would have been in direct conflict with the prophecy Mary had delivered about Him. When Jesus turned down Satan's offer, Satan said to Him, *Then at least prove conclusively that You are the One favored by God. If You won't accept the rulership of*

*all the kingdoms of this world, at least flaunt the fact that You
are God's king. Prove it to everyone.*

Satan escalated the intensity of the temptations of
Christ in an attempt to refocus the call of Christ away
from the poor to the existing power system. These were
temptations to further develop the power systems of this
world, rather than create a new system where the poor
and the hungry were to be favored.

In Luke 4:14 we read the dramatic story in which Jesus
returned to His home town. Jesus purposefully went to
Nazareth where He had been brought up, and waited for
the Sabbath. Then He purposefully went to the synagogue
according to His custom, and purposefully stood up to
read. When the scroll of the prophet Isaiah was handed to
Him He unrolled it and selected purposefully this passage:

> "The Spirit of the Lord is on me,
>   because he has anointed me
>   to preach good news to the poor.
> He has sent me to proclaim freedom for the prisoners
>   and recovery of sight for the blind,
> to release the oppressed,
>   to proclaim the year of the Lord's favor."
>
> (Luke 4:18-19)

My coming, Jesus says, *is good news to the poor, not to the
rich. I am coming to free those imprisoned by the existing
power system.* Then Jesus rolled up the scroll, gave it back
to the attendant and sat down. Every eye in the place was
fixed on Him. At this most dramatic moment He said,
"Today this scripture is fulfilled in your hearing" (4:21).

This was the boy who had grown up in their own little

town. Jesus, looking into their hearts, said, "Surely you will quote this proverb to me: 'Physician, heal yourself. Do here in your home town what we have heard that you did in Capernaum' " (4:23). I believe Jesus intuitively understood their thoughts: *If you are fulfilling this great prophecy of Isaiah and are therefore the Messiah, favored of God, how come you are so poor? How come you are not exalted? Quite obviously people whom God favors are rich and powerful. We want to see some demonstration. Do some miracles and prove your power to us, because your poverty proves you are cursed of God.*

Jesus continued:

> "I tell you the truth, no prophet is accepted in his home town. I assure you that there were many widows in Israel in Elijah's time, when the sky was shut for three and a half years and there was a severe famine throughout the land. Yet Elijah was not sent to any of them, but to a widow in Zarephath in the region of Sidon. And there were many in Israel with leprosy in the time of Elisha the prophet, yet not one of them was cleansed — only Naaman the Syrian." (4:24-28)

The people in the synagogue understood the message: The Messiah had indeed come in the person of Jesus — and had not come for them, but for those they had always believed were cursed of God. They were so offended they wanted to kill Him. But God delivered Jesus out of their hands.

As the text continues throughout Luke's Gospel we notice that Jesus is perfectly consistent with the Scripture He read in regard to Himself. When He wanted to identify the nature of His ministry He picked the Isaiah passage: *I am authenticated because I preach good news to the poor, freedom to prisoners, recovery of sight to the blind, and release to the oppressed. The fulfillment of that Scripture proves that I am God's Messiah.* Throughout the Gospel of Luke we see Him adhering consistently to that principle.

It was the very bottom rung of society that Jesus sought out. Love for those who are rejected was and still is characteristic of Christ. In Luke 4:31, Jesus drives an evil spirit out of someone. To understand the significance of this you have to understand that a demon-possessed person was totally rejected in that society. Jesus goes to Simeon's mother-in-law and touches her because she is sick. Sickness was viewed as a curse from God. From the very beginning, and all through His ministry, Jesus continually went to people with evil spirits and people who were ill. I think the group most comparable in American society to that group of rejected people would be people with AIDS. These are the people Jesus would seek out.

Not the Healthy, Not the Righteous

In Luke 5, Jesus begins to call His disciples by giving them a miraculous catch of fish. He calls Simon, who becomes Peter, then He calls James and John. They were to become His most intimate friends. Their calling came with what was to them a financial miracle. He wanted them to know from the beginning of their ministry that if they would follow Him He would be responsible for their financial situation. If they would follow Him He would assume the responsibility of providing for them.

As we continue, we see Jesus going to the forsaken of His society. He heals a man with leprosy and a paralytic. Then He goes to a tax collector, a person rejected by all the others. Normally a tax collector was in the employ of the Roman government. That alone made him a hated person because he was a collaborator. For a given amount of money, the tax collector would purchase the right to collect taxes in a certain area. In that way the Romans got their money up front and the tax collector earned his profit by collecting back from the people more than he had to pay to the Romans. It's fair to say that a tax collector would frequently prey on weaker people who had no means of defending themselves. He was, therefore, a profoundly hated man.

So Jesus appeared to Levi, who was sitting in his tax collection booth, and said, "Follow me" (5:27). Levi got up, left everything, and followed Jesus. The calling of Levi begins with a turning from money. That was good news to a lot of people because their taxes had already been paid by Levi to the Roman government. Some people were probably standing in line at the booth getting ready to shell out their money to Levi when he disappeared. All of a sudden they no longer had to pay their tax bill.

I remember studying this passage last summer and feeling the impact of what was being revealed to me. I felt enormous relief when I read Luke 5:31, where Jesus said: "It is not the healthy who need a doctor, but the sick. I have not come to call the righteous, but sinners to repentance." I'm grateful for this fact because I am conscious of a deep materialism in my soul that prevents me from being spiritually healthy. This verse says Jesus came for people exactly like me. If you have felt conviction, a sense of sinfulness, in response to this book, remember that this shows you qualify as one of those for whom Jesus came.

Another conflict Jesus had with the proud and powerful was over the Sabbath. The religious leaders had taken

God's kind gift of a day of rest and turned it into an added
burden on the common people.

> One Sabbath Jesus was going through the grainfields,
> and his disciples began to pick some heads of grain,
> rub them in their hands and eat the kernels. Some of
> the Pharisees asked, "Why are you doing what is
> unlawful on the Sabbath?"
>
> Jesus answered them, "Have you never read what
> David did when he and his companions were hungry?
> He entered the house of God, and taking the consecrat-
> ed bread, he ate what is lawful only for priests to eat.
> And he also gave some to his companions." Then Jesus
> said to them, "The Son of Man is Lord of the Sabbath."
>
> On another Sabbath he went into the synagogue
> and was teaching, and a man was there whose right
> hand was shriveled. The Pharisees and the teachers of
> the law were looking for a reason to accuse Jesus, so
> they watched him closely to see if he would heal on
> the Sabbath. But Jesus knew what they were thinking
> and said to the man with the shriveled hand, "Get up
> and stand in front of everyone." So he got up and
> stood there.
>
> Then Jesus said to them, "I ask you, which is
> lawful on the Sabbath: to do good or to do evil, to save
> life or to destroy it?"
>
> He looked around to them all, and said to the man,
> "Stretch out your hand." He did so, and his hand was
> completely restored. But they were furious and began
> to discuss with one another what they might do to
> Jesus. (6:1-11)

In Mosaic law the Sabbath was given as a favor to the
powerless in the world. If it were not for the Sabbath,

slave owners and employers would work people seven
days a week. God understood that men needed a day of
rest so He gave the Sabbath. The religious leaders, interpreting the law, turned the Sabbath into something that
prevented people from being blessed. Jesus challenged
this. On a Sabbath day He looked them straight in the eye
and healed the man with the shriveled hand. He wanted
to elevate their understanding of God's Law from empty,
religious observation to genuine righteousness. God is
never impressed with religiosity. God is always impressed
with true faith. He is offended by people who turn His
laws into mere religious practice so that His laws become
a heavy weight instead of a blessing.

The prophet Amos issued a warning to those turning
the law of God into mere religious practice:

"I hate, I despise your religious feasts;
    I cannot stand your assemblies.
Even though you bring me burnt offerings
        and grain offerings,
    I will not accept them.
Though you bring choice fellowship offerings,
    I will have no regard for them.
Away with the noise of your songs!
    I will not listen to the music of your harps.
But let justice roll on like a river,
    righteousness like a never-failing stream!"

(Amos 5:21-25)

A Prophetic View of Morality

We are far enough along in the Gospel of Luke to begin
seeing the heart of Jesus Christ. He was stunned, shocked,

hurt, and scandalized by people who were suffering. He always turned to help them. The plight of the poor and the sick and the oppressed always moved the heart of Jesus Christ. On this basis we understand that human suffering is what moves and stirs the heart of God.

What the religious leaders did was to take the sense of shock and pain away from the issue of human suffering and focus it onto religious functions. It was a brilliant financial move on their part, because if the issue of morality involves the question of what to do with the poor and needy, it becomes too expensive. But if morality only involves the exercise of religion, then anyone can be perfectly moral but not have it touch their purse.

Legalists are always trying to define morality in terms of anything other than human suffering. In our society we have often made morality simply an issue of sexual purity. This is a far cheaper way to be moral, because if morality is a question of the poor and the sick and the afflicted, then it will touch our checkbook. I want to make it clear that I think sexual purity is very important. In my personal life and in my position of ministry at the Union Rescue Mission I've seen the damaging impact of sexual immorality. Nothing in me would want to weaken anyone's resolve to be sexually pure. I do think, however, that when morality is attached solely to sexuality, as is done too often in the American church, it becomes such an overheated issue that the church cannot help the brother or sister struggling in situations where sexual impurity has become the unmentionable sin, the only recognizable sin.

If I say in some churches, "I sure feel prideful today," they wouldn't worry much about me. If I said, "I feel covetous," they might pray for me. If I said, "I have trouble with my my temper," people would suggest that perhaps I go for therapy. But if I say, "I have a problem with lust," they will give me their harshest judgment.

Again, I agree it is wrong to be lustful, but I don't want to miss the scandal going on in the world through the broader focus of human suffering, for if we miss it, we deny help to those people.

I also need to say that, historically, the poor are more vulnerable to abusive sexuality than others in our society. And the most vulnerable people of all — unborn babies — are hurt the most by loose sexual morals. Sexual morality is an important issue in the overall scheme of human suffering. I do think, however, that we tend to disengage ourselves from the problem of the poor and sick, and focus on the problem of sexuality, because it is a far cheaper way to be moral. The religious leaders could continue to feel moral as long as they scrupulously obeyed their interpretation of the Sabbath law, and it would not cost them a dime. They could retain their sense of being ethical while walking right past people who were poor, sick, and destitute.

God is looking for people who have a prophetic view of morality, who will not defend the brutalization of poor people by the rich in wars whose fundamental goal is the preservation of the position of the wealthy. I sometimes wonder if the American phrase, "Keep America safe for democracy" doesn't really mean, "Keep me rich." We need to examine what we are doing with our armaments and military might. We need to carefully examine how we are treating the poor in our own society, and the poor throughout the world. We need a broad prophetic morality that is concerned about all moral issues.

The evangelical church has expressed its view of morality and the world has declared, *Your morality is too*

narrow. I think that is a fair accusation. The moral viewpoint we Christians have expressed concerns itself almost
exclusively with sexual immorality and that which
springs from sexual immorality — abortion, for example.
While we remain firmly against sexual sins and sins that
revolve around substance abuse, we need to include in
our view of morality the needs of the poor. Until we do
that we are not truly moral.

Blessed Are You

Continuing in Luke:

> One of those days Jesus went out into the hills to pray,
> and spent the night praying to God. When morning
> came, he called his disciples to him and chose twelve
> of them…[then] He went down with them and stood
> on a level place. A large crowd of his disciples was
> there and a great number of people from all over
> Judea, from Jerusalem, and from the seacoast of Tyre
> and Sidon, who had come to hear him and to be
> healed of their diseases. Those troubled by evil spirits
> were cured, and the people all tried to touch him,
> because power was coming from him and healing
> them all. (6:12,17-19)

The picture is that Jesus spent the whole night seeking
the face of God because He had to make a very important
decision — He needed to pick his apostles. To understand
what is occurring here in the hearts of the apostles, you
have to remember that this great healing service was "Act
I, Scene 1" in their training. This is the first ministry-train-
ing experience they'd had. This is one of the places where

Scripture says Jesus healed everyone — He healed them all. People were dancing who had never been able to walk; others were shouting to people who had never heard the sound of voices; some were weeping because for the first time they saw the faces of their children; those who had been brutalized by demons were set free. The noise level and the excitement level must have been tremendous.

The disciples, like others of their generation in Israel, were most likely full of hope for a military solution to the national problem. Their emotions were raging and surging; these were all anointed men, powerfully moved. They were saying, *Surely this is the Messiah! Moses delivered us out of Egypt, Joshua conquered Canaan, David made the kingdom strong; now a new deliverer has come — Jesus.* They were looking wondrously at each other, and watching the people rallying around Jesus. Their excitement was growing. They were thinking, *What an army we'll be! Surely all our dreams will be fulfilled.* Some may have thought, *Maybe I'll get to be Secretary of Defense, or Secretary of State. Just think, Jesus prayed all night and then chose me to be one of His apostles.*

In the midst of all this emotional turmoil and excitement Jesus looked away from the crowd, turned to his disciples, and began to teach them:

> "Blessed are you who are poor,
>   for yours is the kingdom of God.
> Blessed are you who hunger now,
>   for you will be satisfied.
> Blessed are you who weep now,
>   for you will laugh.
> Blessed are you when men hate you,

when they exclude you and insult you
and reject your name as evil,
    because of the Son of Man."

                        (6:20-22)

    In this passage Jesus is not talking to the crowd but to those He had called to be His apostles. This is clearly different from the Sermon on the Mount recorded in the Gospel of Matthew, which Jesus addressed to the crowd. In those days there were no VCR's or tape recorders, so it's not surprising that He repeated the same message in several places. When Jesus addressed the crowd, composed mostly of the poor and afflicted, the people who were drawn to Him, He said, "Blessed are the poor in spirit" because He was aware that not every poor person had the spirit of a poor person. He was saying to them, *If you love money as a rich man loves money, then you do not have a poor man's spirit; you will have problems with Me.* But this is not what He is saying to the disciples. He is not saying you ought to be poor in spirit. He is saying, "Blessed are you who *are* poor, for yours is the kingdom of God."

    As evidence in the Luke passage that He was not talking to the crowd but to the disciples in a ministry focus, at the end of this section He compared the disciples to the prophets. He told them, *Those whom God has used to speak His messages have always been hungry, always weeping, always ill-treated.* Jesus was saying, *See that crowd out there? Their need will dominate your life; therefore, their needs are going to make you poor. Their need for food is going to bring you hunger. You will weep when they weep. And you will be rejected, because people who genuinely speak for God are always rejected.*

In effect Jesus was saying, *Did you come to Me to make you rich? You did the right thing. I will make you rich in the long run. But for now, following Me means poverty. Did you come to Me thinking that I was going to guarantee you a full stomach? You did the right thing. I'll do that, but for now you'll go hungry. Did you come to Me to make you happy? You did the right thing because I will make you deliriously happy, but for now you're going to experience the misery of the people for whom I came. Did you come to Me for fame and power? You did the right thing. Ultimately, in My kingdom I'll make you very powerful, but for now you're going to know what it feels like to be rejected and defamed.*

Now I have to say that preaching the kingdom of God has not done those things to me. And to be honest, I don't know what to do with what I'm reading in Luke. I don't know how to repent, but I will say that one of the most encouraging things I see at this point in the history of the American church is that we are finally getting some opposition. One of the reasons we have been able to preach the gospel with no price tag attached is because we really haven't preached against the sins of our society. Now that we are standing with one voice on issues such as pornography and abortion, society is beginning to oppose us. If we continue to speak for righteousness, particularly as we begin to defend the rights of the poor, we will find opposition.

The Kingdom of the Poor

Then Jesus turns His message around. Again He is not talking to the multitude. He is talking to people who have been called to speak for God. Historically, people who have spoken in behalf of God have suffered for that privilege. Jesus said, *There is nothing in My calling that changes any of that.*

> "Woe to you who are rich, for you have already received your comfort. Woe to you who are well fed now, for you will go hungry. Woe to you who laugh now, for you will mourn and weep. Woe to you when all men speak well of you, for that is how their fathers treated the false prophets." (6:24-26)

We are speaking the message of the kingdom of God into the domain of Satan. If we lack opposition from him, we should be disturbed, for that gives us too much in common with the false prophets. If the gospel makes us wealthy and comfortable, we should be concerned.

As I write this, Union Rescue Mission is planning a new building. As far as public image goes, rescue missions are like jails. Everyone agrees they are necessary, but no one wants one next door. As we attempt to relocate our building, and as we have encouraged others to do things for the poor in other communities, there is always opposition. Yet directly across the street to the east of the mission, an expensive apartment complex and hotel building is being erected. The city welcomes this with open arms, but they want the mission to move.

Arguing against the mission locating in their particular neighborhood, people say, "We don't want that kind of people here; our property values will go down." I'm old enough to remember hearing those exact words used to argue that black people ought to be kept in the ghetto. I believe the American church must take the forefront and charge that those kinds of laws and zoning practices, and the kinds of restrictions that don't allow facilities for the poor, are corrupt and immoral. Everyone has a right to a place to sleep. If the only place a poor person has to lie down is on the sidewalk, then he ought to be able to sleep on the safest sidewalk available. Don't start to tell me that he's on the streets because he's a drug addict or because he's made bad decisions, because in my own middle-class neighborhood I'm surrounded by people who have substance abuse problems, people who have made bad decisions — and *they* have warm beds and houses.

My argument is this: If it's legal for someone to build temporary housing for the rich, like a luxury hotel, in the neighborhood, then shouldn't it be legal for someone or some organization like Union Rescue Mission to build temporary housing for the poor? If it's legal to put up buildings for the rich, like expensive condos, then it ought to be legal in that same neighborhood to build low-cost apartments for the poor.

In actuality, this discrimination against the poor is racial prejudice one step removed. Go to any expensive hotel and count the minority people who walk in. The vast majority of wealthy people, people coming and going from fine hotels, are not the Hispanic and black minorities who have been ravaged by ethnic and racial prejudices in our society. This discrimination is sustained in the way our zoning laws work, in the way building permits can be appealed, and in other legal processes.

Now suppose the body of Christ rises up to defend the rights of the poor in opposition to the rich of this country. We may find out that those who genuinely preach the gospel to the poor become poor themselves. And those who genuinely oppose people who horde resources and keep them from people who need them will become hungry themselves. Part of our responsibility to speak for

God is to speak the full message of God against all oppression and against things that make people sick. If we begin to speak for the oppressed and afflicted and participate in the elevation of these people at the expense of those who are arrogant, powerful, and rich, we will experience opposition such as Christ anticipated for His disciples.

Although I do not know how to repent all at once of my love of money, I desire to make Jesus my Lord, and this has implications for my ability to meet my own needs, my ability to protect my own emotions, and my ability to protect my high standing in my community. I must seriously take into account these implications. Those of us who are committed to interpreting the Bible literally need to interpret these verses in Luke literally. We need to let Jesus' words sink in: "Blessed are you who are poor, for yours is the kingdom of God." Luke's key message is that the kingdom of God is the kingdom of the poor.

As we continue through the Gospel of Luke we'll hear Jesus saying again and again, *The kingdom of God belongs to the poor; and those want to be a part of it must lay their own resources down for the sake of the poor.* Jesus is king of the poor. They may not accept Him as king, nor find Him as Savior, but He is nevertheless their defender.

Finding Security

For those who have money, following God will be costly. Luke gives us these words of Jesus:

> "But I tell you who hear me: Love your enemies, do good to those who hate you, bless those who curse you, pray for those who mistreat you. If someone strikes you on one cheek, turn to him the other also. If

someone takes your cloak, do not stop him from
taking your tunic. Give to everyone who asks you, and
if anyone takes what belongs to you, do not demand it
back. Do to others as you would have them do to you.

"If you love those who love you, what credit is that
to you? Even 'sinners' love those who love them. And
if you do good to those who are good to you, what
credit is that to you? Even 'sinners' do that. And if you
lend to those from whom you expect repayment, what
credit is that to you? Even 'sinners' lend to 'sinners,'
expecting to be repaid in full. But love your enemies,
do good to them, and lend to them without expecting
to get anything back." (6:27-35)

Jesus sets up a logical progression: First, love your enemies; second, do good to them; and third, lend to them
without expecting to get anything in return. If you are to
be a servant of Jesus you will love people; if you love
people you will do good to them; and if you do good to
people it's going to cost you money. That is His basic
expectation of those who will follow Him.

What Christ is saying to us does not make sense unless
we believe in heaven in a very practical way. He says that
whatever we spend of cash resources on earth will be
repaid abundantly in heaven. Our reward will be great
and we will be sons of the Most High. He teaches us that
to give to the poor is to loan to God, who charges Himself
outrageous interests rates. He overwhelms us with financial reward. God's response to our giving away money on
earth will be that He will give back in abundance, out-
weighing any sacrifice we might have made.

In my wallet I have two twenty dollar bills, a ten and
two one dollar bills. Why do I have that money? It is

because God is willing to financially bless such wicked and ungrateful people as George Caywood. The prosperity I enjoy is not mine because I am good, but because of God's grace. Everything that is mine — my family, my education, my fifteen years at the mission — is mine by God's grace. I need to understand this so when I meet wicked and ungrateful people in the world, I'll remember that my Father wants to bless those people just like me. Then I will not refuse to help them just because they may be wicked and ungrateful.

Jesus says in Luke 6:36, "Do not judge." Do not judge whom? The poor. As you decide whether or not you're going to lend, expecting nothing in return, don't make your decision in a spirit of judgment. Do not condemn and you will not be condemned. Forgive and you will be forgiven. Forgive who? The poor. Don't think to yourself, *Their sins have put them in this position.* Forgive them, and then you will be forgiven your sins. Jesus goes on:

> "Give, and it will be given to you. A good measure, pressed down, shaken together and running over, will be poured in your lap. For with the measure you use, it will be measured to you." (6:38)

Here Jesus brings the issue straight back to the primary point: money and its relation to people who are going to speak prophetically for God. *The measure you use to do what?* To give to the poor. Jesus is saying, *Do not condemn people in need, do not judge. Instead, forgive people in need and give generously to them because your personal financial security depends on the fact that your heavenly Father will treat you exactly the same way.*

How do I want God to treat me financially? I hope to

keep my house. It's a nice house. I hope to maintain a car. Therefore, if I want God to continue to bless me, despite my sin, then I must be willing to bless other people in the world despite their sin.

Jesus concludes this discussion with powerful arguments. In Luke 6:40, He says, "A student is not above his teacher, but everyone who is fully trained will be like his teacher." Jesus abandoned the wealth of heaven to bring us salvation. If we are to be like Him we must learn to be willing to abandon our wealth, as our Teacher did.

Then Jesus says, "Why do you look at the speck of sawdust in your brother's eye and pay no attention to the plank in your own eye? How can you say to your brother, 'Brother, let me take the speck out of your eye,' when you yourself fail to see the plank in your own eye?" (6:41-41). Which brother? The poor brother. It is the same discussion as in the earlier verses.

Finally, we have the parable of the wise and foolish builders.

> "Why do you call me, 'Lord, Lord,' and do not do what I say? I will show you what he is like who comes to me and hears my words and puts them into practice. He is like a man building a house, who dug down deep and laid the foundation on rock. When a flood came, the torrent struck that house but could not shake it, because it was well built. But the one who hears my words and does not put them into practice is like a man who built a house on the ground without a foundation. The moment the torrent struck that house, it collapsed and its destruction was complete." (6:46-49)

The wise man is the man who digs through sandy soil on hot days, getting rid of anything which is not solid until he comes to the bedrock. If you do not practice Jesus' command to share your wealth with the poor, you are building your house on sand. It won't stand in the storms and snarls of this world. Jesus is calling us to pick up a shovel and start digging in the softness of our lives, until we have learned to repent over our love of money, until our lives are built on bedrock. If what feels like security to you is not built on the rock, you are in a precarious position.

In living for the poor, I want to rid myself of all that is unstable and all that is soft and all that is shifting, and build on the Rock of Christ Jesus. Once my house is well founded, let the storms of life come, let the sunny days come. No matter the circumstance, my house will be solid.

If you, right now, are wondering about your own level of materialism, and perhaps beginning to feel uncomfortable, I remind you again of Jesus words in Luke 5:31 — "It is not the healthy who need a doctor, but the sick. I have not come to call the righteous, but sinners to repentance" He didn't come for people who are healthy, He came to call wicked materialists like you and me. He is not calling people who read this book and still feel righteous. He is calling sinners to repentance.

GENUINE MORALITY

WHEN ONE OF MY DAUGHTERS was in high school, she toured a major university on visitation day and came back to me saying, "Dad, it's incredible! There must be fifty clubs I can join — all trying to help people." Then she added, "But the kids get loaded and drunk, many of the girls have had abortions, and it seems like most of them sleep around."

I said to her, "Honey, remember that church we used to go to (and I named the church) that had a very high view of sexual morality and a very high view against substance abuse; but had no concern for the poor?" I reminded my daughter what James had written: "For whoever keeps the whole law and yet stumbles at just one point is guilty of breaking all of it" (James 2:10). The bank robber who is sexually pure is still an immoral person. The person who sleeps around, but is generous and honest with money, is still an immoral person. To break any part of the law is to break all of the law.

"Which is the more moral institution?" I asked her, "the church or the school?"

She said, "Dad, I see your point. Neither institution is really moral. They are just immoral at different points."

The morality Jesus lived and taught was a total morality. It was concerned with fleshly appetites *and* the needs of the poor. Anyone who lives and teaches a lesser morality is morally deficient.

Seeing God's Response

As we resume our journey through Luke, we find Jesus entering Capernaum.

> There a centurion servant, whom his master valued highly, was sick and about to die. The centurion heard of Jesus and sent some elders of the Jews to him, asking him to come and heal his servant. When they came to Jesus, they pleaded earnestly with him, "This man deserves to have you do this, because he loves our nation and has built our synagogue." So Jesus went with them. (Luke 7:1-6)

The fact that the centurion was willing to commit his funds to the things of God motivated Christ to meet his need. A similar thing happened in Acts 10 with Cornelius. Cornelius had a hunger for God, so an angel was sent to him with this message: "Your prayers and gifts to the poor have come up as a remembrance before God" (Acts 10:4). Like the centurion, Cornelius found that his willingness to give money to the poor generated a response from God. In the case of Cornelius it was a very dramatic response. As a direct consequence of his actions, the whole nature of Peter's ministry changed. Peter became the door-opener for the Gentiles into the church

Because Cornelius was a Gentile, it required something supernatural on God's part to bring him salvation. This suggests that not only is there no repentance unless you repent about money, but when you repent over money you can expect a response from God. Just like every other Christian, Cornelius was saved because he trusted Christ as his Savior and because of Christ's work on Calvary. However, his willingness to give to the poor opened the way for this salvation to come to him.

In Luke 18 we read the story of the rich young ruler, a Jewish leader who apparently had an attractive and regal bearing. He was respected and seen as a good man, a man blessed of God, a likely prospect for following Jesus.

Zacchaeus, in Luke 19, was just the opposite. He was a hated Roman collaborator and he was small in stature — so small, in fact, he had to climb a tree in order to see Christ. He certainly did not want to risk getting into a mob of people, as hated as he was. This fact necessitated that he run ahead of the crowd. Zacchaeus seemed an unlikely prospect for repentance.

When the rich ruler heard Christ's exhortation to "Sell everything you have and give to the poor" (18:22), he became sad because he was a man of great wealth.

> Jesus looked at him and said, "How hard it is for the rich to enter the kingdom of God! Indeed, it is easier for a camel to go through the eye of a needle than for a rich man to enter the kingdom of God." (18:23-25)

But when Zacchaeus was confronted by Christ, he immediately gave half of his possessions to the poor. The other half he would use in his act of repentance. Mosaic law required anyone guilty of cheating to pay back his victim in full, plus one fourth of that amount. Zacchaeus, who had cheated many people, said, "I will pay back four times the amount" (19:8).

In contrast to the rich young ruler who would not repent because of his wealth, Zacchaeus laid his money at the feet of Jesus.

> Jesus said to him, "Today salvation has come to this house, because this man, too, is a son of Abraham. For the Son of Man came to seek and to save what was lost." (19:9-10)

The position of these two stories near the end of the narrative and before the events leading to the crucifixion and the resurrection act as a summary of Christ's teaching in this Gospel. Their position gives weight to one of Luke's central messages: Failure to repent about money is no repentance at all.

Certainly in the American middle class — with our powers of communication, our ability to travel, the luxury and comfort we enjoy — all of us can consider ourselves wealthy. I think it would befit each of us to think of our repentance and salvation from this point of view, to safeguard our walk with Christ.

Not Just Any Beggar

Another revealing account in Luke is the parable of the rich man and Lazarus, a sore-covered beggar. Lazarus was starving to death and longing to eat what fell from the rich man's table, if only he were allowed to. Then he died and went to Abraham's bosom. The rich man also died and went to the place of torment.

It was not the rich man's failure to help the hungry in faraway lands that brought damnation upon him, but rather his failure to help Lazarus, the beggar who lay at his gate and over whom he had to step each time he came and went from his home.

It is commendable that Christians care for people in distant places. The apostolic work of Paul in raising funds for the poor, particularly in Jerusalem, illustrates our obligation to relieve the suffering of people we don't know. But that alone is not sufficient. We also have the responsibility to minister personally to those right next to us. We are accountable for the people whom we, in fact, stumble over as we live out the course of our life.

In Jesus' story the rich man becomes the beggar, longing for a drop of water to cool his tongue. But he was refused by Abraham.

> "He answered,'Then I beg you, father, send Lazarus to my father's house, for I have five brothers. Let him warn them, so that they will not also come to this place of torment.'
>
> "Abraham replied, 'They have Moses and the Prophets; let them listen to them.'
>
> " 'No, father Abraham,' he said, 'but if someone from the dead goes to them, they will repent.'
>
> "He said to him, 'If they do not listen to Moses and the Prophets, they will not be convinced even if someone rises from the dead.' " (16:27-31)

The rich man's brothers would fail to repent not because of lack of evidence, but because of the condition of their hearts. They would not have done what was necessary in order to introduce the possibility of God coming into their lives. Each year Union Rescue Mission sends out hundreds of thousands of letters to people who are not supporters. We ask them to consider giving to the poor through the ministry of the mission. For those who are not Christians, this introduces the possibility of bringing them to repentance over money and ultimately bringing them to an encounter with Jesus Christ.

This Lazarus parable is most unusual because it mentions a name. It is not just any beggar, it's Lazarus. So Jesus may have been describing the eternal situation of a rich man and a beggar everyone knew about. Perhaps Jesus was saying that Lazarus could have been a guide through the eye of the needle of salvation for the rich man who couldn't get through on his own.

If the rich man had one day stopped and looked down at poor Lazarus and said, *Man! I don't know what to do about your physical condition, seeing how ill you are, but I certainly can bring you into one of the bedrooms and help you stay clean and make sure you have food to eat,* it may have led to an encounter with Christ.

A Different Christ

Returning to Luke 7 we see the continuing effort of Christ to reach the poor and the oppressed of this world. We recall that when He went back to his home synagogue in Nazareth, He said He was being called to the afflicted and poor and imprisoned of this world. It is not surprising at all that as we follow the narrative of Christ through the Gospel of Luke we witness His encounter with exactly those kinds of people again and again.

Jesus met a widow who had endured the loss of her husband and was facing the loss of her son as well. Jesus was deeply moved by her grief and solved her problem. He cured many with diseases and gave sight to many who were blind. It was an ongoing part of His ministry.

The disciples of John visited Christ and wondered, "Are you the one who is to come or should we expect someone else?" (7:18). Jesus offered this evidence that He was the Messiah: *The blind receive their sight, the lame walk, those with leprosy are cured, the deaf hear, the dead are raised, and the good news is preached to the poor.*

Then He added a rather chilling comment: "Blessed is the man who does not fall away on account of me" (7:23). In other words, *The level of repentance I am demanding from you in regard to the poor may drive you away from God.*

As I studied the Gospel of Luke, I encountered a different Christ from the one I thought I knew. I have encountered a Christ deeply concerned about the love of money in His followers and a Christ who focuses on people in need. I have encountered a Christ who says to me, *The kingdom of God belongs to the poor. The poor are under God's blessing, not His curse. The kingdom of God belongs to them. If you would like to participate in this kingdom you are free to, but the level of repentance necessary for entry is willingness to repent about your money.*

If I am unwilling to be made poor for the sake of the poor then I am unwilling to repent about anything. So I am blessed if I do not fall away from Christ on account of His uncompromising message about the poor.

In Luke 7:29-30, there is a parenthesis with this commentary: "All the people, even the tax collectors, when they heard Jesus' words, acknowledged that God's way was right, because they had been baptized by John...." The common people, even the hated tax collectors, knew Jesus was from God and that what He was saying was

Truth. How? Luke says they knew it because they had been baptized by John. The rest of the parenthetical statement continues, "But the Pharisees and experts in the law rejected God's purpose for themselves, because they had not been baptized by John."

Why did the religious leaders and the legal experts reject God and His purpose for their lives? Because they had not been baptized by John. The challenge of John's preaching was this: "Produce fruit in keeping with repentance" (3:8). When asked what that meant, John required that people repent over love of money to the exclusion of repenting over any other sin,

I'm sure John's logic was that if they repented at the level of money, all other repentance would come automatically. To the people who repented about money, John said, *All right, I see fruit worthy of repentance, I'll baptize you on that basis.* Then when Christ came, their hearts were prepared to hear His message.

On the other hand, the religious leaders and the experts in the law had refused to repent about their money and were not baptized, so when Jesus came they claimed He was the antichrist.

This remark about the Pharisees in Luke 7:30 is the most chilling Scripture I have ever read in my life: *They rejected God's purpose for themselves...* How many people in the Christian community have rejected God's purposes for their lives because they've refused to repent about money?

One of the surprising things I have discovered in my walk with Christ, particularly in the early days, is how *good* the will of God is. The last thing most real Christians want is their own way. If you walk with Christ for any length of time you're scared to death of having it your way. You want His way. This thought that the failure to repent about money results in a rejection of God's purpose for our lives is terrifying.

Losing Life

As the story of Jesus continues in Luke 7, we find Him being anointed by a sinful woman, illustrating again that it was those who needed forgiveness who came to Him. Moving on to chapter eight we see a number of the extremely oppressed of this world being touched by Christ: a demon-possessed man, a dead girl, and a woman subject to chronic bleeding. It was the rejected and forgotten of the world to whom Christ paid attention.

In chapter nine, Jesus sends out the twelve disciples. It is no surprise that as part of their training He tells them to take nothing for the journey: no staff, no bag, no bread, no money, no extra tunic. Jesus was committed to the idea that all who followed Him would be accustomed to the idea of depending on God to supply their needs. They are serving the Good King, and the Good King takes care of obedient subjects.

When they returned, Jesus was confronted by five thousand people and He fed the entire crowd. Five thousand ate and were satisfied, leaving twelve baskets of food to be picked up by the twelve disciples, one basket for each of them. Those who would serve God and His Christ need to learn to depend on God to be their source.

In Luke 9:19 and the following verses, we have Peter's confession of Jesus as the Christ. We know from other Gospels that immediately after this confession Jesus began to predict His own suffering. Peter protested. His protest may have been based on the opinion that talking about suffering was not a good way to gain new recruits. Jesus

responded to Peter in a way we all must hear. Following
Christ necessitates pain.

> Then [Jesus] said to them all: "If anyone would come
> after me, he must deny himself and take up his cross
> daily and follow me. For whoever wants to save his
> life will lose it, but whoever loses his life for me will
> save it. What good is it for a man to gain the whole
> world, and yet lose or forfeit his very self?" (9:23-24)

What we have here is a picture of the most successful
materialist the world has ever known. The richest person
living on earth gains only a small portion of the world, but
Jesus is suggesting the logical extreme. Even if someone
gains the whole world, he will find it of no value whatsoever if, in the process, he loses his own soul.

Life insurance salesmen confuse me because they have
so many alternate plans and different ways to be covered.
But when Christ makes His call He does not have plan A
for the serious Christian and plan B for the less serious.
He said: "If *anyone* would come after me, he must deny
himself, take up his cross daily and follow me." There is
no doubt in my mind that He was talking, among other
things, about the necessity of being willing to deny oneself
personal wealth.

> As they were walking along the road, a man said to
> him,"I will follow you wherever you go."
>   Jesus replied, "Foxes have holes and birds of the air
> have nests, but the Son of Man has no place to lay his
> head."
>   He said to another man, "Follow me."
> But the man replied, "Lord, first let me go and bury
> my father."

...Still another said, "I will follow you, Lord; but first let me go back and say good-by to my family."

Jesus replied, "No one who puts his hand to the plow and looks back is fit for service in the kingdom of God." (9:57-62)

Jesus was not speaking in parables. These are actual people who turned their backs to Christ, at least in part, because He was not a man of wealth, not a man with even modest means. He lived and worked simply, without a place to lay His head. That made it hard for people to follow Him. If He was worth following, surely He would be rich. While the general public was inclined to follow the rich, Jesus saw things differently. To Him the wealth of the greedy was not a reason to elevate them but a reason to disclaim them.

In Luke 11:39, Jesus chastised the religious leaders: "Now then, you Pharisees clean the outside of the cup and dish, but inside you are full of greed and wickedness." In other places and times Jesus was content to sum up a problem with the word "wickedness," but here again He picked out the word "greed." He singled it out from all other sins and identified it. Wickedness covers many kinds of sin. Greed is a specific sin, and Jesus was emphasizing here its devastating character. He goes on to say, "You foolish people! Did not the one who made the outside make the inside also? But give what is inside the dish to the poor, and everything will be clean for you" (11:40-41). Here again He says, *Do you want to repent? Give what you have to the poor and then you will be clean from the inside out.*

For the Sake of Security

The parable of the rich fool is found in Luke 12. The rich fool believed that because of his prosperity he did not need God, so God required his soul. The two things he wanted in life were security and pleasure: "And I'll say to myself, 'You have plenty of good things laid up for many years. Take life easy; eat, drink and be merry' " (12:19). Pleasure and security are the primary motivations of greed. Money becomes idolatrous because only in God can we know true security, and He is the originating source of all pleasure.

At the birth of time, Adam and Eve enjoyed absolute security and perfect pleasure, those things the rich man only imagined were his. When Adam and Eve sinned, they were removed from the garden — their "place" — and forced to live in an insecure world where they had to labor very hard and find in that their pleasure. We all long to return to the ideal situation of Eden. That, of course, is one of the reasons for coming to Christ. We want to go to heaven, to live in an eternal paradise. But some people believe money gives them the power to return to Eden while remaining in rebellion to God. They think their wealth will once again give them security and pleasure, this time without a judgmental God.

The challenge Christ lays before His people is to learn to be rich toward Him instead of storing up things for themselves. He issues a challenge to choose between saving money to spend versus investing money in heaven. When we choose Him, heaven can reach back to us here and now with its peace and joy.

"And do not set your heart on what you will eat or drink; do not worry about it. For the pagan world runs after all such things, and your Father knows that you need them. But seek his kingdom, and these things will be given to you as well.

"Do not be afraid, little flock, for your Father has been pleased to give you the kingdom." (12:29-32)

Jesus tells his disciples not to worry about food and clothes. "Your Father knows that you need them," He says. *Seek My kingdom, and the necessities of life will follow.* Christ's message is to those of us whose lives are full of possessions. He wants to elevate the discussion above just food and clothing, because God is willing to give us the entire kingdom. In a sense the followers of God are the ultimate materialists. They stand to gain God's entire kingdom.

"Provide purses for yourselves that will not wear out, a treasure in heaven that will not be exhausted, where no thief comes near and no moth destroys. For where your treasure is, there your heart will be also." (12:33-34)

There is no security in the money you invest in this world. When Jesus talks about treasure in heaven, He's talking about money. In other words, Jesus is suggesting that you take care of your real future, your eternity. To the rich Christian He would say, *Do not end your financial planning with your retirement. Include eternity in your plans and make yourself wealthy in heaven with lots of spending power.*

We remind each other, *You can't take it with you!* But, oh yes, you can! Jesus wants you to! He wants you to put your cash in heaven. That's the point He's making when

He says, "Where your treasure is there will your heart be
also." He's not talking about emotional riches or spiritual
riches. He's talking about money. If your money is in this
world then your heart is in this world. But you *can* send
wealth on ahead.

We try to manage Scripture by spiritualizing it; be rich
toward God emotionally, be rich toward God spiritually.
That's not His point. His point is to make yourself rich by
means of giving to the poor. We have tried to take money
out of this formula because if Jesus is talking about financial wealth it will change the way we spend the cash in
our wallet today. When Jesus said, "Your Father has been
pleased to give you the kingdom," He is not issuing some
heavy sentence. He is offering real pleasure and absolute
security in the kingdom of God.

The kingdom of God is like packages under the Christ-
mas tree! Jesus is saying, *Ah, come on. Live it up! Sell every-*
thing you have, give it to the poor. Then watch what God will
do for you. Watch how God will make your life secure and make
your life happy in this world. And He'll make you incredibly
wealthy in the next.

Jesus is not laying some heavy condemnation trip on
us. That is not His point. Instead, He is inviting us to a
secure life, a peaceful life, a joyful life. And He is offering
us a chance to make ourselves incredibly rich in the next
life. His message is, *If you don't do it this way, if you don't*
put your cash in heaven, you're going to end up poor in the
next life. If you put your cash in heaven, your heart is going to
follow it there and that's going to bring order and peace and joy
into this life. I doubt if heaven includes a system of currency, but we can exchange our worldly currency for the
unspoilable wealth of heaven.

If you were before a group of people seated in a room

and you asked all of them who read the stock report in this morning's paper to stand up, and then asked all those who had money invested in the stock market to raise their hands, the people who stood up would be the same people who raised their hands. Likewise, if your investments are in heaven your attention will be toward heaven. Paul wrote, "Set your minds on things above..." (Colossians 3:2). Jesus had already explained how to do this: by putting your treasure there.

Proverbs 19:17 says, "He who is kind to the poor lends to the LORD, and he will reward him for what he has done." This is the lesson Jesus is trying to teach in Luke 14:12. Jesus tells his host not to invite friends, brothers, relatives or rich neighbors when he gives a luncheon or dinner, for they might invite him back and then he would be repaid. "Invite the poor, the crippled, the lame, the blind," He tells him. *Then blessings will follow.*

So when you give to a poor person you are lending to God. All throughout Scripture we are forbidden to become loan sharks. The fact of the matter is that God does allow us to lend at scandalous, outrageous interest rates! He's looking to make that kind of loan from His people as we give to the poor.

Speaking of Dollars

Also in Luke 14 we are challenged by the parable of the great banquet. There were three excuses mentioned for why people could not come to the banquet. Two of the three excuses were built directly around finances, again illustrating the message in Luke that the opponent of repentance is wealth. Virtually all of those who repent in Luke's Gospel repent about money.

In the parable of the prodigal son a son is tempted away from his father by money. "Give me my share of the estate," he demanded. And he went away to have a good time. Finally, his money ran out and he came to his senses.

> "How many of my father's hired men have food to spare, and here I am starving to death! I will set out and go back to my father and say to him: Father, I have sinned against heaven and against you. I am no longer worthy to be called your son; make me like one of your hired men." So he got up and went to his father. (15:17-20)

The boy's father was looking for him and saw him coming from a long way off. The son began getting ready the little speech he had carefully rehearsed: "I have sinned against heaven and against you ...Make me like your hired hand." His speech was interrupted by the love of his father. It's hard to give a speech when you're being swept off your feet with a hug and smothered in kisses.

This story is very comforting to me. Christ is saying that if I am willing to begin to repent about money and turn back toward God, I will find that He is searching for me and I will not have time to give my little speech of repentance before I am overwhelmed by His love and affection.

Before the son's speech was over the father began giving directions: *Bring the best robe, put a ring on his finger and sandals on his feet! Let's have a party!* If we are willing to turn away from materialism, we will find that He is pursuing us and has already prepared for us security and pleasures no amount of money can buy.

In Luke 16 is the unusual story of the shrewd manager.

A wealthy man had hired the manager, who then was accused of wasting the wealthy man's money. The manager, afraid he would soon be fired, gave large discounts to people who owed his master money; in one case a fifty-percent discount and in another a twenty-percent discount. In this manner he won many friends for himself. The master commended him for his shrewdness in using resources that were not his own, but over which he had been called to manage, to prepare for his own future. Jesus is saying that if we are wise, we will use the resources God makes available to us to prepare for our future. "I tell you, use worldly wealth to gain friends for yourselves, so that when it is gone, you will be welcomed into eternal dwellings" (16:9). This suggests that God has given us everything we have. Everything under our management ultimately belongs to God. Jesus is encouraging us to be as smart as this shrewd manager and use the resources at our disposal to prepare for our eternal destiny.

In Luke 19:11-26, we have the parable of the ten minas. The master in this story gave each of his servants a measure of money. He then instructed them, "Put this money to work." Each servant was later rewarded proportionately to the investment he had made. I am glad the New International Version does not translate the ten minas as ten *talents*. For in our efforts to manage the shocking demands of Christ in regard to money, we have taken the word *talent* — which was simply an ancient measure of money, like a dollar — and turned it into a *gift or ability* because we do not want to deal with what Jesus actually said. He was saying, *I have given some of you a lot of money, some of you less money, and some of you a little money, and I expect you to make good, sound investments.* He was not speaking of your ability to sing, your graduate education, or your gift of public speaking. He was speaking of your dollars. If you do not responsibly invest your dollars for the kingdom of God you are like the last fellow in the story who received only one mina and did not invest it, because he was afraid of the master. Therefore even his one mina was taken from him.

The parable of the ten minas is clearly a call to invest our earthly riches in our eternal future. Failure to make that investment means the loss of even what little (as compared to the enormous riches of heaven) we had on earth. When we willingly make investments in heaven, earthly issues become clear to us. Jesus made the same point in Matthew 6:22-23.

> "The eye is the lamp of the body. If your eyes are good, your whole body will be full of light. But if your eyes are bad, your whole body will be full of darkness. If then the light within you is darkness, how great is that darkness!"

Where you put your money is where you focus. If you are not focused on eternity, the inevitable consequence is that you will be filled with darkness. What does that mean? Someone filled with darkness doesn't like himself. He is filled with fear, and tends to say, *I must be careful, otherwise I won't measure up.* He is full of doubt — *How can God love me when I'm such a sinner.* He is full of bitterness — *My lane on the freeway is always the slowest.* He's full of resentment — *Why didn't God give me that promotion that I wanted? I'm depressed, I'm trapped, I'm pinned down in a situation I don't like but can't escape.*

If I do not love and trust God enough to invest my money in eternity I will inevitably serve mammon;

because where my money is, my heart is. If I want my heart to be focused on eternity, I'm going to put my money there. It's that simple. If I am involved in making myself richer and richer in terms of this world, my heart will inevitably follow my money; my concern will be for this world, and that familiar grim darkness will invade my soul.

Free to Enjoy

Christ goes on to say:

> "Therefore I tell you, do not worry about your life, what you will eat or drink; or about your body, what you will wear. Is not life more important than food and the body more important than clothes? Look at the birds of the air, they do not sow or reap or store away in barns, and yet your heavenly Father feeds them. Are you not much more valuable than they? Who of you by worrying can add a single hour to his life?
>
> "And why do you worry about clothes? See how the lilies of the field grow, they do not labor or spin. Yet I tell you that not even Solomon in all his splendor was dressed like one of these. But if that is how God clothes the grass of the field which is here today and tomorrow is thrown into the fire, will he not much more clothe you, O ye of little faith? So do not worry, saying 'What shall we eat?' or 'What shall we drink?' or 'What shall we wear?' For the pagans run after all these things, and your heavenly Father knows that you need them." (Matthew 6: 25-32)

Jesus is saying, *Don't make your decisions on the basis of what you can afford. There's more to life than food and clothes.*

Make your decisions on the basis of what is right. If at the mission we sought to do only the things we could afford, we wouldn't make all the progress we are making. When we see a situation that needs to be addressed we say, *God, we're going to start pushing on the door, and if You close it, that's fine, because what You want is important.* But we are not going to decide on the basis of how much money we have that the door is already closed. We're going to decide on the basis of what's right, what we ought to be doing, what the will of God is. Life becomes an adventure. If my wife and I had decided only to have the children we could afford, we wouldn't have any children. It's been a long time since I've met anyone who could *afford* to have kids. People who wait until they can afford to have kids many times end up not having them, but people who have kids find a way to support them by the grace of God. God is calling us to another kind of life — a free kind of life.

Suppose when my kids were little they came running in the house with a package of bologna and a loaf of bread saying,"We mowed lawns in the neighborhood to buy food because we were afraid you wouldn't give us lunch." I'd just be heartbroken if they'd had that fear. What I wanted to hear from my kids was confidence in me and anticipation of what I was going to provide for them. When they went to bed at night, I didn't expect them to ask, "Daddy, are you going to give us breakfast in the morning?" I wanted them to sleep well all night and to enjoy their lives and to learn and develop and grow and leave breakfast and lunch and dinner to me. I would take care of it. I was committed to it.

Jesus said, "Except you...become like little children you will never enter the kingdom of heaven" (Matthew 18:2). All He is asking from us is to trust like little children. He's saying, *Let Me make you free. Let Me make you like a child, so you're free to grow and achieve and be happy. And don't worry about tomorrow, I'll take care of it. Leave those problems with Me.*

It's not as if He's giving us some big, heavy burden we must bear; *Oh, we have to give our money away, how awful!* Not in the least. Rather, He is calling us to be like a child so we're free to enjoy life. By giving to the poor we give evidence to Him that we really trust Him with tomorrow, and that we refuse to worry — because we trust our heavenly Father day after day, one day at a time.

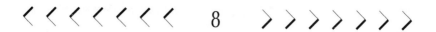

WHEN JESUS REFUSED TO FEED THE HUNGRY

AT UNION RESCUE MISSION, resources are available that are sometimes denied to a person who would like them. For example, anyone who has been on the street long enough knows the mission's meal-time system. If they are not on time they miss out on that meal. Every organization, no matter how small, must have structure. But we have a policy that "no one gets caught in the cracks." The goal of the mission is to meet needs. If someone has a need that our structure is not allowing us to meet, then virtually anyone at the mission has a right to violate the system in order to meet the need.

The other side of that coin is that we do not want to be irresponsible. If someone refuses to be there at the right time to receive a service, we ask them to wait until the next time that service is offered. We must do this to avoid promoting an irresponsible lifestyle. If you attempt to meet every need a street person presents, you end up being what the Alcoholics Anonymous people call an *enabler*. An enabler encourages people to remain in a self-destructive lifestyle by removing all the painful consequences of that lifestyle. The mission, and anyone who sees himself in a helping ministry, must be careful not to be drawn into that role.

Lunch with a King

John 6:1-9 illustrates an important principle affecting anyone who will try to help people. I've come to call it the "Five Loaves, Two Fish " principle.

> Some time after this, Jesus crossed to the far shore of the Sea of Galilee (that is, the Sea of Tiberias), and a great crowd of people followed him because they saw the miraculous signs he had performed on the sick. Then Jesus went up on the hillside and sat down with his disciples. The Jewish Passover Feast was near.
>
> When Jesus looked up and saw a great crowd coming toward him, he said to Philip, "Where shall we buy bread for these people to eat?" He asked this only to test him, for he already had in mind what he was going to do.
>
> Philip answered him, "Eight months' wages would not buy enough bread for each one to have a bite!"
>
> Another of his disciples, Andrew, Simon Peter's brother, spoke up, "Here is a boy with five small barley loaves and two small fish, but how far will they go among so many?" (John 6:1-9)

If you start out to meet the needs of the world, you sense constantly that your resources are hopelessly inadequate, just as this boy's lunch was inadequate to meet the vast needs of the crowd. At the mission, for every ministry opportunity we accept, we turn down fifty because of the limit on our resources. Learning to deal with that, and to depend on God to somehow make our inadequate resources adequate, becomes very important.

What would have happened if the boy had refused to give his five loaves and two fish to Christ? Would the multitude have been fed? The answer is no. The boy could easily have said: *Well, what's the use? It won't do the multitude any good. The only result will be that I will go hungry, that I won't have lunch.* But apparently he was a boy of faith because he willingly risked going hungry for the sake of giving his lunch to Christ. Christ, taking this small lunch, made it adequate for the great crowd of people, with plenty left over.

The result of Christ's action was that the crowd wanted to make Jesus king, and wanted to do it by force because so many of these people lived close to the edge of hunger. They saw a potential in Christ to meet one of the most basic human needs, the promise of adequate food. Jesus refused to allow this to happen.

The next event we see is Christ walking on the water. The disciples went across the lake by boat and Jesus went out on the water to meet them. In this action I think Jesus was saying, *While I will not allow the crowd to make me a human king I do want you to know I am God. Moses parted the sea, I walk on the sea. I demonstrate my divinity by showing my dominance over the elements.*

This is characteristic of Christ. He will never allow Himself to be elevated to the top of human institutions of power. He always insists on the establishment of His own kingdom. There is no evolutionary progress from the governments of this world to the kingdom of God. The economic systems of this world can never be gradually improved until they become the kingdom of God. It is always a revolution, an imposition. Ultimately, Christ will violently destroy the kingdoms of this world. That is one of the basic messages of the book of Revelation. He is leader of an opposing kingdom. We belong to His invading army. We are in His advance contingent force.

The Problem of Breakfast

The next morning the crowd of five thousand faced a problem. Though they had enjoyed a great meal the day before, now they wanted breakfast. Obtaining breakfast became their goal. I have a habit of overeating on Thanksgiving — in fact, I can make myself absolutely miserable. (I suspect this may be a universal fault in our country.) I hear myself saying after the Thanksgiving meal, "Boy, I'll never want anything to eat again." Then Friday morning comes. I don't remember ever missing breakfast on the Friday morning after Thanksgiving. This was the problem the crowd faced. They went looking for Jesus in order to have breakfast. When they found Him on the other side of the lake they asked, "Rabbi, when did You get here?"

Jesus answered, "I tell you the truth, you are looking for me not because you saw miraculous signs, but because you ate the loaves and had your fill" (John 6:26). He was saying, *Yesterday I put up a billboard, a sign, but you did not read it. That miraculous feeding was the sign, but you are not coming to Me because you read the sign and are now genuinely interested in Me. No, your only concern is to refuel your stomach.* Jesus had a goal of His own. He wanted the people to understand that He was God and that in Him all the provision of God was made available to man.

A few years ago I lost confidence in my ability to supply adequately for my family. I was looking at the expenses of college and weddings, of eight more years of needing a relatively high income for raising a family. I just didn't think I was going to be able to pull it off. It really frightened me. I tried to comfort myself with the scriptural assurances that God provides for His children. Questions arose in my mind: "If you loved me Lord, then why did you let me go hungry as a child?" I could not accept the comfort of God. My faith was shallow because of the memories of being without food.

I prayed some very anguished prayers. Then the Holy Spirit responded within my spirit, saying, "You made it, you survived, you're here with relatively good health." I began to reflect. I remembered from my childhood a righteous man named Mel who drove a bakery truck. He was willing for some reason to give our family credit. Sometimes on the Sunday just after a Friday payday — especially if it were the week we paid rent — we ran out of money. But Mel was always there with his loaves of bread, his cherry pies and his brownies. That's not ideal food, but we did eat.

As I reflected on my situation, I understood that God had filled my life with provisions. He gave me parents, and He put me in a very large, rich church with plenty of resources. It was His will that my need be fully met. But my father was consistently unable to put food on the table, and this eventually led to his suicide. The church did not reach out to help us. A congregation of well-to-do families allowed my family to suffer. As I thought about this, God said to me, *Now, that was not good that the church would not help and that your father committed suicide. That was not good, but I made it work for you. You were dealt a poor hand of cards, but I played it skillfully and well, and I made it work for you.*

I had to reinterpret my childhood to understand the reality that God had always been with me. One particular experience helped me. I took my own children to see the home of my childhood in Tucson. I had remembered every detail about that house. It had an L-shaped porch that went across the front and down one side. It had a vacant lot next door with oleander bushes. The memory was so vivid. But I was shocked when I looked at that big house. It had turned into a tiny seven-hundred-square-foot cottage. And the huge lot next door was now only a small patch of dirt. I had to adjust what I had remembered from my childhood to what I was seeing as an adult. Because I had been small, the house had seemed large. Now I was able to evaluate the size of that house in a true perspective.

This helped me understand my need to go back and reinterpret my personal history; in effect, to reread the billboards from an adult point of view. God did not expect me to understand anything as abstract as Himself when I was a little boy. But God did expect me to reread the billboards now, just as Jesus asked of the crowd He had fed the previous day.

I remembered that while growing up I felt very alone. But as an adult I have gotten a truer perspective. The truth is that I haven't been alone a single second of my life. Yes, I have suffered, but I have never been alone in my suffering. As I've reexamined the events of my life, I've discovered a loving God and I'm hungry to know that God. I've found Him to be faithful and kind and wise, and fun at a party!

What happened to me through hunger and poverty and my father's death threw me into a pit. Through many decades of trying to crawl out of that hole I've learned a great deal. If this book means something to you, remember that it came out of tragedy. If what I do for the poor at the Union Rescue Mission in Los Angeles is significant, it is because of that tragedy. If I have been a good husband and a good father, it is because of what I've learned from the Holy Spirit while coming out of that tragedy. If the messages I've preached in churches have meaning for people, they and I owe it all to God, who helped me deal with the earlier tragedies that marked my life.

'You've Got the Provider'

Jesus told the crowd in John 6,

> "Do not work for food that spoils, but for food that endures to eternal life, which the Son of Man will give you. On him God the Father has placed his seal of approval." (6:27)

The crowd of people responded, *Now you're talking our language. You want us to work for our breakfast. That's only fair. We'll do that.*

Jesus answered, "The work of God is this: to believe in the one he has sent" (John 6:29). For the sake of what they truly needed, He refused to give them the food they wanted. Their real need was Himself. Everything else was incidental.

My wife and I have a friend who is a very fine artist. He painted several pictures that we value highly. In the bedroom of our former house he painted a great mural. It had a castle in it and a number of suns around the castle indicating the course of the day. The sun went into the moon — it was just an incredible piece of art. When it became clear that we were going to move I went to him and said, "Paul, I don't know what to do. I just can't leave that painting." He laughed and said, "Forget the painting, you've got the painter!"

Jesus was saying to the crowd, *Don't worry about provision; you've got the Provider. Don't worry about what you're going to have for breakfast or what clothes you're going to wear, because you've got Me. You'll never have to worry about breakfast, or lunch, or dinner again.* Their response was, *What miraculous sign will you give then, that we may see it and believe You? What will You do?* What did they want, a bolt of lightening across the sky? Did they want Him to go back out and walk on the water? No, they had a particular sign in mind. They said, "Our forefathers ate the manna in the desert; as it is written: 'He gave them bread from heaven to eat' " (John 6:31). They were trying to negotiate with Him. *Okay, you prove to us that You are God. And by the way, a nice way for You to do that is to give us breakfast. Then we will believe.*

> Jesus said to them, "I tell you the truth, it is not Moses who has given you the bread from heaven, but it is my Father, who has given you the true bread from heaven. For the bread of God is he who comes down from heaven and gives life to the world." (John 6:32-33)

Once again Jesus makes Himself the issue. Up to this point they have been wanting breakfast, but now they say, *Sir, from now on give us this bread. Not just breakfast; we like the sound of this heavenly bread. Give it to us from now on so we can take early retirement and not have to worry about things so much.*

Jesus said to them, "I am the bread of life. He who

comes to Me will never go hungry, and he who believes in me will never be thirsty" (John 6:35). That is an easy verse to spiritualize; to say *spiritually* hungry and *spiritually* thirsty. But there is another issue involved, the practical matter of food and clothes. If you come to Jesus as the Son of God, as the king, and you are His faithful subject, then the king will take care of you. He will meet your needs. He is a good king. Now, if you rebel against the king you are in another situation. But good kings take care of good subjects. It is a mistake for us to spiritualize this verse and say we will never go hungry *spiritually* and never be thirsty *spiritually*. That may well be implied here too, but Jesus was fundamentally dealing with their physical hunger and physical thirst. He was offering them the only way possible in the world to ease their load of anxiety. They were saying, *Give us this bread on a permanent basis*, and Jesus was saying, *I am willing to give you Myself on a permanent basis.*

That does not preclude the possibility that some of God's children will die of starvation. Some died on crosses, others by stoning. The story of the death of Stephen in Acts 7 says that Stephen forgave his murderers while he was being stoned to death. He was able to do that because of the intensity of the presence of Christ. He saw heaven opened and Jesus standing at the right hand of God. Normally, Jesus was seated at God's right hand, but while Stephen was suffering, Jesus stood up. He was unable to remain seated at that sacred moment. We may live to see the day when, for righteousness' sake, some Christians will starve to death. But the suffering will be dominated by the joy of the presence of Christ, and after that will come the comfort of heaven.

Jesus used the parable of the workers in the labor pool

(Matthew 20:1-16) to illustrate for the disciples the concept of Himself as Provider. In this parable the master gave a full day's work to some and only a few hours work to others, but paid all of them the same wage. Many people in ancient times lived hand to mouth, day to day. Some days they had food, some days they didn't. The drama of this parable was that the people who didn't work, didn't eat. So it was a great relief at the eleventh hour when the master came back to the marketplace and offered them work. That meant the possibility of buying a little food for themselves and their families. To their surprise and delight he paid them as much as those who had worked all day. Jesus is saying, *I am the Provider. I am the only way out of this life of anxiety. Follow Me, be willing to be last, and I will give you the comfort and the security you long for.*

Eternal Breakfast

Back to the narrative of the multitude who wanted breakfast — Jesus refused to yield to the pressure of the crowd for another miracle. "For my Father's will is that everyone who looks to the Son and believes in him shall have eternal life, and I will raise him up at the last day" (John 6:40). Jesus extends their view again. They were saying to him, *Give us this bread from now on, for the rest of our lives,* and He replied, *It is better than that. If you will accept me as the Son of God, I will take care of you well beyond this life, throughout the everlasting ages that are before you into the next life. Because I am the eternal breakfast that comes down from heaven. All you need is Me.*

There are two things we need to get clear from John 6. The first is: Set your eyes on Christ, and anything else you need will follow. The second is: Even Christ at times made the hard choice not to feed hungry people. It is important to me that I do not abuse this principle and use it to excuse my own laziness or greediness, but I need to know that Christ, for the sake of eternal values, sometimes refused to meet people's physical needs.

This takes the pressure off me. I do not feel obligated simply to respond to whatever need presents itself. Instead I can walk in the Spirit and respond to human need in light of eternal principles.

THE CROSS IS A CHOICE

THE CROSS is at the heart of the kingdom of God. It was the cross of Christ that gave entrance for the love of God into the world. It is your cross and mine that make His love available to our world. The failure of Christians to be cross-bearers has brought tragic results.

By *cross-bearers* I mean Christians who will participate in the suffering of the afflicted in the name of Jesus Christ. Cross-bearing, unlike tribulations, which are the common lot of all mankind, is suffering we take upon ourselves in order to bring the love of God to others. Distinct from humanitarian acts, cross-bearing is done in the name of Christ.

The first principle of cross-bearing is that it is not optional. Christ said, "If anyone would come after me, he must deny himself and take up his cross, and follow me" (Matthew 16:24) To attempt to design a pain-free relationship with God built on exciting Christian activities can give a semblance of spiritual vitality without inconvenience. When Christian activities become replacements for cross-bearing they lead to emptiness.

The root of the problem is that we contemporary Christians are trying to use our money to create a way to have the dynamic of a walk with Jesus Christ without the necessity of pain. We have become hung up on hype and high-powered entertainment in our worship, as well as a style of preaching that generates a sense of excitement, but bypasses the inconvenience of the crucifixion. The world sees through us and our attitude.

We do not need more famous TV evangelists. We need more Mother Teresas. It would be a healthy sign in this country if it was possible to phone *The Los Angeles Times* about some woman living in voluntary poverty in south-central Los Angeles, pouring her heart out for the people down there, and hear the editor say, *Well, what's newsworthy about that? That's just another one of those crazy Christians laying down their lives for the poor. There are thousands of those. That's no story.* The only weakness with Mother Teresa is that she's newsworthy.

The American church is trying to design a satisfying, joy-giving, peace-giving Christian walk that does not involve the cross. We have made it possible to hide from our pain, to hide from our sin, to hide from our need because we're rich and have so many things. We allow our money to bring us comfort. We live in hiding, so we have gotten out of touch with reality.

One time Jesus met a blind man. He took him outside the city and with His spit healed his eyes. Jesus said, "Do you see anything?" The man replied, "I see people. They look like trees walking around" (Mark 8:22). Isn't that a great image? In other words, he couldn't see very well. His sight was improved, but it certainly wasn't the vision he had hoped Jesus Christ would give back to him. Then Jesus touched him again and he saw all things clearly. I think our need for a Savior has introduced us to the salvation and forgiveness of Jesus Christ, but too often, we see the things of God as trees walking. Our vision is blurred.

The body of Christ is caught in a no man's land between "not quite blind" and "can't quite see." The children of Israel came out of Egypt and wandered in the wilderness on their way to the Promised Land. Those years were difficult, painful, empty and necessary, but they weren't God's perfect plan. God wanted to call His people out of the wilderness and into the Promised Land. We have defined and created a wilderness Christianity, because of the risks inherent in the cross that we are trying to avoid. There's no joy, no peace, and no love among us to draw the unsaved. In the absence of these we have created all kinds of high-powered sales techniques and we have abandoned the cross. We see the things of God as trees walking.

Isaiah, speaking of Christ, says, "See, my servant will act wisely, he will be raised and lifted up and highly exalted" (Isaiah 52:13). We're drawn to that kind of living — the raised and lifted up and highly exalted kind of living. We're drawn to that, but we don't read on to the next verse: "His appearance was disfigured beyond that of any man, and his form marred beyond human likeness" (Isaiah 52:14). That's the cross. The last twenty-six chapters of Isaiah are basically saying there is another kind of living God calls us to. The joy of life, the vitality of salvation, and the peace of God come to those who are willing to gain them through suffering.

Isaiah 53 begins: "Who has believed our message?" I think it was Maxwell Smart who used to say, "Would you believe?" I don't think the American Christian population has believed Isaiah's report that the way to exaltation in the kingdom of God is straight through the pain of the cross. Who wants to believe that?

I want to speak the truth to you, but I don't want you to feel condemned. That sense of condemnation, that sense of shame, is the enemy of what I'm calling you to. Paul says it this way in Romans 12:1 — "I beseech you therefore brethren, by the mercy of God, to present your body as a living sacrifice." There is a great temptation to say, *I beseech you therefore brethren by the justice of God*. If God is just, we owe Him our sacrifice because He gave everything for us. If you are living in fear of the holiness and justice of God you will not be able to present your body as a living sacrifice. Although you may experience salvation, if you allow your heart to feel condemned you won't be able to walk in and obey the Holy Spirit.

I have tried to persuade you of the compassion of God because I understand that when we as individuals begin to base our life on the mercies of God, we'll be *able* to present our life as a living sacrifice. If a woman is married to a man who always does everything right and is tremendously pure, but who has no sense of mercy, will she be willing to lay down her life in wifely love for him? I don't think so. She won't trust him. *If I give my heart wholly to this man*, she would say, *why, he would demand sacrifices of me that I couldn't make. I could never live up to his standard. I am too afraid of him to do that.* If a woman is persuaded of the compassion of her husband toward her, then she is in a better position to lay down her life for him. If you are afraid of God, you won't lay down to die in His arms. You won't allow yourself to be crucified.

The second principle of the cross is that it is always a choice. You must choose to die on a cross, it is never imposed on you. There are many difficult things in life over which you have no control, but those things are tribulations. Everyone has trials and tribulations. We are clearly told in Scripture that they result in benefit, but they are not the cross. The cross is always something you choose.

The cross of Christ was not imposed on Him. He accepted it as an act of obedience. In John 18, when the soldiers came to arrest Him, He said, "I Am," which is the name of God. When Moses asked God for a name He said, "I Am that I Am is My name." So when Jesus looked at these soldiers and said, "I Am," they fell over like dead men. He had revealed His true nature as God. Their finite natures could not endure this. He gave them another chance, asking, *Who did you say you were looking for?* Having made the point that others had absolutely no power over Him, that He could simply walk away if He wanted to, Jesus said, *Okay, now you can arrest Me, but you have got to let the disciples go. I am choosing to allow you to arrest Me, but only on My terms.* The soldiers dutifully released the disciples. Jesus was clearly the dominant figure. Was He a victim? Not a chance!

Jesus Christ does not want you to be anybody's victim. Not of your husband, not of your wife, not of your employer. He is calling you to lay down your life so you might experience His resurrection. The cross is always a choice. It is not optional, it is always painful, and it is always a choice. *Lord, I see that person in need, I choose to involve myself in that person's life. It is going to bring me pain, but I choose for the sake of redemption to get involved.*

The third principle of the cross is that it always reveals the truth. It is like an onion. Jesus went through the events of the crucifixion with dignity: sleepless for two nights, a couple of kangaroo trials, deserted by his friends, beaten,

spit upon, mocked, paraded naked through a city, and
finally nailed to the cross. The cross was lifted from the
ground and dropped into a hole. The weight of Jesus'
body tore against the wounds in His hands and feet. He
hung there for many hours. We are told that death on a
cross causes the crucified to endure the agony of suffoca-
tion. So to improve the ability to breathe, he shifts his
body weight to hands and feet. But he cannot take that
long, and goes back to suffocating again. Christ went
through hours of that. Layer after layer after layer of
Christ's heart was being peeled away, and truth was being
revealed as only words of love fell from His lips.

Jesus speaks, worried about His mother. He said,
"John, here is your mother." No sin there. The agony gets
greater and greater and greater and He asks without accusation, "My God, my God, why have you forsaken me?"
No sin there. He looks upon those who are abusing and
torturing Him and says, "Father, forgive them, they do not
know what they are doing."

At any point He could have called for legions of angels
out of heaven to deliver Him. I am sure the angels were
anxious. I am sure their swords were sharp. I am sure they
were dividing up the crowd between them. I am also certain the angels were bewildered. As Jesus opened His
mouth just before He died, they must have felt, *This is our
call, this is it! He is going to call us to battle. Let's go down
and get us some Roman soldiers.* One angel might have been
thinking, *You can have the soldiers, but those gawking religious leaders over there, they are mine!*

Jesus opens His mouth and says, "Father, forgive
them, they do not know what they are doing." The angels
put their swords away. They recognize there is going to be
no warfare that day. To the very end there was nothing but

love and holiness in the pure heart of Jesus Christ. Obviously, it was not for His own sins that He endured the cross.

How different it is for humanity. When we take up the cross, our own sinfulness is revealed as the layers of our defenses are stripped from us. Over the years as I have attempted in the name of Jesus Christ to bear the pain of others, my own sin has been revealed to me. I have begun to see my needs clearly. But what God reveals, God heals. So I have learned to look for crosses for myself, because it is by means of the cross that I find healing for the agonies of my experience. Lustful, arrogant, ambitious, gluttonous, dishonest as I am, I find victory over sin on the cross. Sin I am unaware of is revealed to me there. I want that to happen. It is painful, yes, but I choose to introduce the cross into my life because I am going to become free from the power of wrong.

Part of the incorrect understanding American Christians have is this: *We come together, we meet together, we minister to each other, and then when we've got it all together we will go out to the poor and the sick and the afflicted in the world and bring what we have discovered to them.* That will never happen. If the church remains inside its walls, Christians will never be healed and changed. Healing happens only by taking up the cross daily. It is in the process of bearing pain that we are changed. As the pure heart of Jesus Christ was revealed on the cross, our sinful hearts are revealed there also. Until our sins are in the open they cannot be dealt with, and we cannot be healed.

The fourth principle of the cross is that it is never a sacrifice. It was said of Jesus, "He will see his offspring and prolong his days, and the will of the Lord will prosper in his hand. After the suffering of his soul, he will see the

light of life and be satisfied" (Isaiah 53:11). Jesus could
have said to God, *Let me get this straight. If I go to earth as a
man, live in sinlessness, go through all the agony of the cross, I
get to spend eternity with George Caywood?* If the Father had
responded, *That's the deal,* Jesus would have said, *I'll take
it! It's worth it to me.*

Jesus took up the cross because He wanted to. In
Hebrews 12 we read of "Jesus, the author and finisher of
our faith, who for the joy set before him endured the
cross." Your cross has to be borne for the joy set before
you just like Jesus bore His.

If I go to a street person at Union Rescue Mission in
order to bear his pain, and I do it as a personal sacrifice,
then what I get out of it is a religious feeling. *Boy, I'm religious! Man, am I spiritual!* That is not pretty. That is ugly,
hideous self-righteousness. If I go to an individual out of a
sense of my own need, looking for Jesus, looking for the
Christ in him, it is different.

We must remember that when Jesus told the parable of
the good Samaritan He did not identify with the good
Samaritan. He identified with the beaten and robbed man.
And He said, "Whatever you did for one of the least of
these brothers of mine, you did for me" (Matthew 25:40).

Jesus is most available to me — if I am hungry for
Him, if I am starving for Him, if I need His peace, if I need
His healing — in the broken and humiliated people of the
world. He makes Himself available to us through them.
Are you hungry for Jesus today? Are you tired of being
victimized by your sin? Are you tired of being angry and
full of rage? You can find all the help you need when you
come to Christ as He is found in the poor and afflicted.

I need that help too. I read in the Bible that I was created to have dominion over everything God made, but I

am struggling to have dominion over my own body, never mind anything else. Jesus said, *The gates of Hades will not overcome the church.* I don't have time to worry about the gates of Hades because there is enough hell going on within me. I am tired of seeing the power of God, and the joy of God, and the peace of God as trees walking. I want to see clearly.

I need that man lying on the sidewalk in front of Union Rescue Mission because in him I find Jesus. I don't come to him because I've got something he needs. How ugly could I be? I come to him because he needs Jesus, and so do I, and in him I find Jesus.

But there is something even better. After crucifixion there is a resurrection. Jesus gave this concept its definition. He said, "I am the resurrection" (John 11:25). As I take the pain of others upon myself and experience crucifixion, I begin to look for the risen Jesus Himself. That is the best part. When you allow the crosses in your life and you get to the other side, what do you find? The resurrection: *Jesus.* This process, applied daily, will lead us out of our emptiness, into another reality. This is the theme of the parable of the treasure buried in a field.

> "The kingdom of heaven is like treasure hidden in a field. When a man found it, he hid it again, and then in his joy went and sold all that he had and bought that field." (Matthew 13:44)

The man went "in his joy." He didn't say, *Boy, do I hate to sell this 4 X 4 pickup.* He was glad! Whatever it took, whatever he had to sell to buy that field with the treasure in it, he was glad to do.

A friend of mine painted an incredible portrait of

Christ in four panels. The first time I looked at it I was stunned. My friend said, "George, I want to sell you this painting."

"Paul," I said, "it's a masterpiece. I can't buy it; you need to keep it. It's tremendous."

"But I *want* to sell it to you," he said. He kept insisting, but I kept refusing.

A few months later Paul came back to me saying, "George, I really need money and I want to sell you that painting." He listed a price and I wasn't able to resist. I pulled out my wallet, but I wasn't thinking, *Oh, how I hate to part with this money!* No, I handed over the money with great joy. There was no sense of sacrifice in it.

> "Again, the kingdom of heaven is like a merchant looking for fine pearls. When he found one of great value, he went away and sold everything he had and bought it." (Matthew 13:45-46)

No sense of sacrifice here. A cross is an exchange of values. You are giving something of little value to get something of enormous value. There is no sacrifice in it. The cross of *religion* is a sacrifice, but the cross of Christ is taken with joy because you know that on the other side you'll find Jesus.

One of the most romantic things I have ever read is the statement in Hebrews 12:12 that Jesus endured the cross for the joy set before Him. You and I are the joy of Christ. For Him it was worth going through the cross in order to have fellowship with you and I throughout eternity. There, on the other side of the cross of Christ, was *His* joy: you and me. And the reverse is true: On the other side of *our* cross, our joy is waiting; that is, Jesus. We go through the cross for Him just like He went through the cross for us. How romantic could anything be?

I have hinted at this but I want to make it clear: Our cross in this world is people who are hurting. Lazarus, the beggar, lay at the door of the rich man. Why? To bring the rich man to salvation. There were poor people in the pathway of Cornelius and he helped them. The angel who came to Cornelius said to him, "Your prayers and your gifts to the poor have come up as a remembrance before God" (Acts 10:4). God heard his prayers and sent Peter to tell him about salvation. If the rich man had helped Lazarus, it would not have brought the rich man salvation (that would have been salvation by works), but God would have opened to the rich man the possibility of salvation instead of damnation.

If you are looking for a cross, look in your neighborhood for someone with AIDS, someone who is going through a divorce, someone who is depressed or mentally ill, someone who is hungry or homeless or afraid. Some people reading this will say, "Wait a minute. I am that person. I am the one in need." This may be true. Each one of us may become someone else's cross. If you are my cross you open up possibilities of salvation for me. But the fact that you are in pain or difficult circumstances now does not mean you should wait for someone to come to you. You should go to someone else in the meantime. The world is filled with millions and millions of crosses. Just open your eyes.

You cannot choose *everybody* who needs help to be your cross. You can't make yourself responsible for every problem in the world or in your city. But at least one or two people in your life stand with outstretched arms, saying, *Someone help me!* They've put their body in the shape of a cross. They represent to you a marvelous opportunity to encounter Jesus Christ.

Jesus says, *Look for a cross every day. Look for someone in pain, look for someone in need. Take this person's pain upon yourself. Endure that cross.* Clearly, people who are upset are upsetting, troubled people are troubling, miserable people create misery. You bear the trouble, not with any sense of martyrdom, but because in the act of meeting the need of that person you encounter your own personal resurrection, which is Jesus Christ.

And say, *I take this cross with joy. Yes, with joy! This is my moment. I'll have to go through a little pain, but I'm going to meet Jesus — and I'm hungry, hungry for Jesus.*

Have You Thanked Him for Your Lunch?

AS DIRECTOR of Union Rescue Mission I am sometimes asked the hard question: "If God is so loving, why are people starving to death in Africa?" Whenever I am asked this, I respond: "Have you thanked Him for your lunch?" If you are going to blame God for the fact that people are starving to death in Africa, the least you can do is give Him credit that you can eat consistently.

God is the Provider

In Scripture God is clearly the Provider God. He is the God who by His very nature provides. The creation of earth followed this sequence: God created light, then separated the earth waters from the sky waters. Out of the earth waters emerged the dry lands, and on the dry lands the plants grew. To keep track of the seasons and the passage of time, the sun, moon, and stars were created. On the fifth day the sky and sea creatures were made. The land animals were created on the sixth day.

As God progressed, it's as if He paused before He created man and said, *All right, everyone report in.* After He had determined that the earth was complete, and that it was beautiful and wonderful, then, in effect, God said, *Now let's take the best of everything and put it all in one place, the Garden of Eden.* When He had completed the Garden and all the provisions were ready, He created man.

It would have been untrue to His nature to have created man first, then said to him, *Now, sit in that corner while I create a world for you to live in.* No, He provided the most wonderful and perfect environment imaginable. Having completed that, He made man. This is a strong testimony of His nature as Provider God.

As we all know, man sinned in the Garden of Eden, judgment became necessary, and Adam and Eve had to leave the Garden. But before judgment fell on them, God took care of them. He prepared animal skins for Adam and Eve to wear, clothes that would prepare them for judgment. God provided for His creation. And of course, centuries later He would give the world the unspeakable gift — the gift of Christ Himself, the ultimate provision who was sent to prepare creation for the final judgment.

Suppose you had been an angel living five thousand years ago and a committee of other angels came to you and said, *We have this wonderful idea for dealing with the sinner-man. God should send His son as a man to the earth. Then His son must be put to death on a cross as a substitute for man. Now — YOU have been chosen to sell this idea to God.*

Would you want to be the one to suggest such an outrageous idea to God? I wouldn't. Yet God Himself originated the idea. He is by nature the Provider God, so He was willing to endure even the murder of His innocent Son so you and I could be saved. This incredible measure of forgiveness could only be bought by the blood of Jesus

Christ. The Father God — the Provider God — willingly endured the bloodshed necessary to purchase man's redemption.

As we look closely at the issue of starving nations against this image of the Provider God, we must recognize that there is actually plenty of food in the world. The problem is not a lack of resources, but the greedy social, political, and economic systems that prevent a fair distribution of those resources, leaving some people overfed while others starve.

God designed His system so that the human population explosion would coincide with the explosion of knowledge and technology as well. We are still able to produce enough food for everyone, because God made us capable of it through expanding technology. The personal experience of God's people, the history of the earth, and the testimony of Scripture all reveal God to be, by nature, the Provider God.

God's Responsibility

If God is the Provider, that means I am not personally responsible for starving children. God is responsible. The Scriptures teach us to do the will of the Father; our task is to obey. Therefore, after faithfully doing a day's work for Him at Union Rescue Mission, I can go home at night and enjoy my family despite the world of unmet needs on skid row. I am not responsible to meet all those needs. I'm responsible to be a faithful director of the mission, marshaling as many resources as God provides to relieve suffering in downtown Los Angeles. If I have been faithful in that calling, I can sleep well at night despite unmet needs still remaining on the streets.

If I am working on skid row as a do-gooder, what am I to do with myself when I feel I am not doing any good? Everybody who ministers to the desperate needs of this world has a sense that in the long run he is not really accomplishing much at all. It's the same overwhelmed feeling you would get if you tried emptying the ocean with a bucket. If you want to be involved in alleviating the the tragedies that afflict the human race, you have to deal with such feelings.

As the great saints have shown us, when we go to the poor and needy of the world we can deal with these difficult feelings only when we go as obedient servants of Christ, rather than as do-gooders. After all, God is the Provider God, and He is responsible. My task is to be faithful to Him, not to meet the needs of everybody around me.

Failure to consistently live according to the way we were designed to live is to invite disaster. Have you ever said to your kids, "Don't rock back on that chair — it's not a rocking chair"? You're trying to help them understand that a chair can be destroyed if it's used in a way it wasn't designed to be used. If you walk out to the garage and see your child trying to pound a nail with the handle of your saw, you say to him, "If you want to pound a nail, get a hammer." By using a tool in the wrong way, you end up destroying the tool and not getting the job done. It's the same for us: If I'm trying to do a job I wasn't designed to do, I will end up destroying myself, and God's purpose in me will go unfilled.

Years ago, long before I came to the mission, my wife and I ran a halfway house in the San Fernando Valley for drug addicts, alcoholics, and mental patients. We were trying to minister to fifteen or twenty people at a time and had little money. We lived on what we could buy with a Bank Americard at a nearby 7-11 store. At the same time I was attending classes five days a week at Azusa Pacific University in the San Gabriel Valley, an hour-and-fifteen-minute commute each way.

Predictably, I ended up in a hospital bed, confused and bewildered. It didn't look like I was going to be able to graduate, though by then I was in my last semester. I began to pray and spend time with the Lord. He helped me recognize three ways to respond to human need. The first way is to try to make myself responsible for all the suffering I see, and attempt to meet every need. As a mere human being, however, I would only end up destroying myself physically.

The second way to respond is to ignore human need and suffering. But if I do that, I die spiritually. Unfortunately, this is the plight of many of God's people, because they refuse to address the desperate human need all around them.

The third alternative is the happy, life-giving one: to walk in faithful obedience to God's calling for *my* life.

God brought to my mind Christ's rebuke to Martha, who was angry because her sister wasn't helping to prepare dinner. Jesus said, "Only one thing is needed" (Luke 10:42). If I am burdened with one hundred things to do at the same moment, ninety-nine of them aren't from God.

At this moment, while I write this book, the mission's problems are still ongoing — the need to raise money for the new building, the improvement of our programs, the personnel problems. At home I'm still a father, still a husband, the lawn still needs mowing, the garage still needs to be cleaned. The dog probably needs a bath. All the responsibilities involved in being the head of a household

are still waiting. The church where I preach still has its
needs. But I know it is safe for me to ignore all those
responsibilities and give myself happily to the thing God
is asking me to do right now. Only one thing is necessary.

Jesus is not a cruel taskmaster. He does not tell us to
do three or four things at the same time. It's our happy
privilege just to follow Him, to put our hand in His and
walk with Him, to experience the joy of the moment. I
don't always remember to live that way, but when I do
remember I get a lot done. When I meet pressing problems
at the mission — such as an important conference with
someone — I can give myself totally to that person,
because I know God is working on my behalf at home and
in the other areas of my life. I can trust Him to provide for
the other people I'm responsible for. Frequently, without
any effort from me, He will resolve a situation I might
have worried about without my being involved at all. So a
great deal of work tends to get accomplished when I
remember that my father is the Provider God.

To my regret I consistently demand to be in control
myself. If I am to trust God to take care of my family when
I am at the mission and take care of the mission when I am
with my family, then I have to give that up. It is often hard
for me to yield control to God. But the busyness that con-
sumes me is a reflection of my personality, not of the
demands of God. When I walk in obedience, I walk in
quietness and peace.

The Situation Isn't Hopeless

People ask, "Well then, what is the solution? How can we
effectively minister to all the world's needs?" I answer,
frankly, "I don't know." But I do know God is willing to

take the responsibility. If His people bring to Him their five-loaf-and-two-fish lunches, we can solve this thing. We can deal with this problem. It is not hopeless.

The newspapers say relationships in America continue to break down: The divorce rate is still climbing, and there are breaches between parent and child, labor and management, and government and business. We live in a fractured society. This breaking of relationships has produced the homeless situation, and I don't see the situation improving. I see no reason to expect housing costs to stop escalating. And I see no reason to believe America will be put in a better competitive position industrially. I see nothing in the newspapers that gives me hope.

My hope is in God alone. He is the almighty God and He has accepted the responsibility to meet the need. If I am willing to enter the battle with Him, to be used according to His will, there is no need for me to feel hopeless about the situation. I don't have to know all the solutions. If I continue to be faithful to take up my cross daily and follow Him, twenty years from now the problem of homelessness can be licked.

Finding Fulfillment — And Growth

In Romans 3:23, Paul says, "For all have sinned and fall short of the glory of God." At first glance this seems to be a somewhat ridiculous statement. That's like me saying I don't play basketball as well as Magic Johnson (anyone who has seen me play basketball knows this instantly). It's just as ridiculous for me to compare myself with the glory of God. But I think Paul in this verse is trying to help me understand that I fall short of the image of God in me. I am a bearer of part of the glory of God since I was made in His image, but I am constantly falling short of that. This sense of being less than I was designed and made to be is what gives me my sense of shame. I will never be happy if I am not a provider, because I am made in the image of the Provider. If God is the Provider God and I am made in His image, I must participate in His program if I wish to experience fulfillment.

If Christian growth is the process whereby I become more like God, my ability and willingness to provide should grow stronger and stronger as time goes by. A man once said to me, "I have tithed for thirty years." I replied, "If you confess, I'm sure God will forgive you." The man's statement was an admission that for thirty years he had failed to grow in his ability to give. We should expect to see growth, for people who are a part of God's process of provision tend to end up better provided for themselves, like the widow of Zarephath who fed Elijah. She gave her last bit of food. This act opened the door for God to provide for her miraculously.

We have to be careful, however, and not judge the poor in this regard, because there are wonderfully righteous people pouring out their provisions who are still in a time of financial struggle. To say that poverty is evidence of unrighteous living is to make the same mistake the religious leaders made in Scripture. But as a general principle, people who participate in God's program to provide for the needy will find their own needs provided for. A lifestyle of being a provider tends to put you in a financial situation of having more resources to give away. Your ability to give grows on that basis.

A provider lifestyle helps your faith grow too, so you become more willing to take financial risks for God. At one point, you may be willing to give only five percent, but if you have walked with God, depended on Him, and found Him to be faithful when you provided for others, soon you are willing to risk ten percent. In a few years you may be willing to risk fifteen percent. Not only does the pool out of which you participate in God's provision grow, but the depth of your willingness to cut into your pool grows. Your ability to be a provider grows.

My wife Jerelyn has the gift of giving. She knows what to give and when. It's a wonderful gift to see in operation. When I worked in the Azusa Pacific University kitchen we used to make donuts for the students. When they became stale, I was allowed to take some home. Once a plate of donuts had been sitting around our house for a few days and had become thoroughly stale. When Jerelyn saw one of our neighbors out in her driveway, Jerelyn said to me, "God is leading me to give that plate of donuts to our neighbor."

I said, "Honey, those donuts are stale."

Jerelyn replied, "I can't help it. I just feel strongly led to give those donuts to that woman." In my husbandly dignity I thought, *Well, I must allow her this experience.* While Jerelyn took over the plate of donuts, I prepared several nice sermons about how she should be wiser. I was preparing to comfort her in her failure, as a good husband should.

Then Jerelyn came back and said, "Well, I led the lady to Christ. When I walked up with the donuts she said, 'You know, that's the first gift anyone has given me personally in ten years.' She began to weep right there in the driveway."

I packed away all my sermons in my mental filing cabinet, because I could see operating in my wife the Holy Spirit's ministry of giving.

To learn to give with humility is important. It is possible to give in a way that makes me feel superior, which is always humiliating to the recipient. When I was growing up, a woman used to bring groceries by for my mom. Over the years this lady got in a bad position herself, so my mom took a bag of groceries to *her.* The lady said, "Oh, Louella, I can't take those groceries."

Mom looked her right in the eye and said, "Why, all those years I thought you were bringing groceries to me because you loved me. Now it turns out you were bringing groceries to me because you felt superior to me. You really hurt my feelings."

The lady had the grace to reply, "Well, I'm sorry, Louella. That's really proud of me, isn't it? You know, I was very comfortable giving to you, but now that it's my turn, I don't have the humility to receive." That lady repented on the spot and created a warm and wonderful memory for my mom. It is important to give with a humble spirit, and be able to receive when our turn comes around.

In summary, successful Christian living in the midst of human need requires we have an understanding of the following principles:

1. God is the Provider.

2. If God is the Provider, I am not responsible for the situation. I am responsible only to obey Him and do my part.

3. If God is the Provider, the situation is not hopeless.

4. If God is the Provider and I am made in His image, I must take part in the provision process in order to experience fulfillment.

5. If Christian growth is the process whereby I become more like God, I can expect growth both in the quality and quantity of my giving.

WHY SHOULD I HELP THE HOMELESS?

MANY PEOPLE ASK ME, "Why should I help homeless people? Why don't they just go and get a job? After all, every week there are four sections of want ads in the Sunday paper."

The fact is, most of the jobs listed in the Sunday paper require an education, experience, demonstrated skill, and the flexibility to work a particular shift. But when Jesus puts out a want ad He sets different standards:

"Come to me, all you who are weary and burdened, and I will give you rest. Take my yoke upon you and learn from me, for I am gentle and humble in heart, and you will find rest for your souls. For my yoke is easy and my burden is light." (Matthew 11:29)

Sometimes we hear the testimony of a recently converted actor or professional ball player or businessman, and we say, "What a tremendous asset he will be to the kingdom of God." When we indulge in that kind of thinking, we express a radically different point of view from

God's. Christ is looking for the weary and the burdened, as well as those willing to *become* burdened for others.

As Christians, we need to help the homeless because they are exactly the kind of people Jesus is looking for. God has chosen to give His kingdom to the poor. This is one reason why Jesus had so much trouble with the nation of Israel. He came not to represent the Jewish nation, but to represent a kingdom of the poor.

Hopeless Pursuit

To ask, "Why don't homeless people just go get a job?" insinuates that these people are lazy, and would do better if they only wanted to. The question implies, "We work hard for our money; why should we give it to someone who doesn't?" The truth is that homeless people do want to work. Our country is full of people who have been on skid row and used a facility like Union Rescue Mission to put a bottom under their lives, get a job, and escape from homelessness and a dead-end way of life.

For the person who has been homeless a long time, a different kind of reality presents itself. Let's follow one such person, who at the beginning of the day has twenty dimes and one nickel in his pocket. He goes into a grocery store and with two of the dimes and a nickel buys a Monday morning copy of *The Los Angeles Times*. The cost of the newspaper represents better than ten percent of his entire resources. Now he is down to eighteen dimes.

He looks in the want ads and sees a few ads for jobs he might be able to do. He goes to the corner, puts two dimes into a pay phone, and calls the first number. The person who answers tells him the personnel director in charge of hiring for the job is out for the day: "Call back tomorrow."

He uses two more dimes to call about another job. The personnel director there is away from her desk.

He puts in two more dimes to call another number, and is told the job is filled.

He is down to twelve dimes. He puts two of them in the phone and tries once more. This time he is told, "We'll send you some information about the job. What is your address?"

"I don't have an address," he answers.

"Well, I'm sorry, we're not interested. You won't be eligible for this job."

Now he is down to ten dimes and has a decision to make. With ten dimes he can get a cinnamon roll and a cup of coffee at a donut shop, and sit there for a few hours reading the rest of the paper. Or he can continue to drop those dimes into the phone in the seemingly hopeless pursuit of a job.

If you're looking for work but have a home and telephone, you can endlessly dial job number after job number. But if you're on the street with extremely limited resources that are rapidly being used up day after day in what seems to you a futile effort, you begin to conserve those resources for other purposes.

If you do get a job interview, it requires a tremendous cost. You might have to give a pint of blood to get bus fare for the trip from downtown Los Angeles to West Covina (provided the business is close enough to the bus line). You might do this, that is, if you can find a place to get a clean shirt and clean pair of pants, and if you have managed to find a place to sleep so you are rested enough to feel like going to a job interview.

If you actually make it to the interview, but then are turned down for the job (something we have all experienced), then from your point of view you have used your valuable resources for nothing.

If you happen to have a background of mental illness, the situation becomes even more bleak — the want ads become a source of self contempt. If you are confident and think you have some job skills, you pick up the want ads and they offer you hope. But if you are insecure and afraid, looking through four sections — not four pages, four sections! — of available jobs makes you begin to hate yourself, because you may not see even one job you think you can get. Those want ads become a source of great condemnation. You start to think, *What kind of guy am I? There must be three or four thousand jobs listed in this paper and I'm not qualified to do even one.*

Wanting a Different Life

This sense of hopelessness about employment creates a misunderstanding between homeless people and those who stop and casually offer them help. Middle-class people almost always want to tell me their horror stories: *I stopped my car and tried to help this person and they didn't want to work. I think people are homeless because they prefer it. Don't all those people down there on skid row like that kind of life?*

When I'm asked such a question it's my pleasure to answer, "I've never met anyone who prefers that kind of life." But I've met a lot of people who think they cannot live any other way, and have made some kind of adjustment, refusing to hope. When you go to a person like that and offer him a job, his fear rises and he thinks, *Oh no, I'll fail again. I'll have something for a few days and then I'll be back out on the street.* So he says to you, "I don't want to work. I like it down here." Yet I have repeatedly seen despairing and angry and hostile people begin to plan and to work — once they are given a realistic belief in a different kind of life.

How many homeless people prefer to be on the streets? I say, none do. How many have adapted to life on the streets? Virtually all of them. But if you personally begin to give an individual hope, they will make enormous sacrifices to escape the very unpleasant life of homelessness.

I once told these things to an audience, and the principal of a Catholic girls school stopped me afterward. "George," she said, "I know exactly what you are talking about. Over and over again we have kids tell us they hate school. 'I don't want to be here,' they say. 'I don't want to learn. I'll never use what I learn here anyway.' But if those students get in the hands of a great teacher who bypasses their fears and instills self-confidence in them, you begin to see achievers who *want* to be in school. I have to kick 'em out at night so the teacher can go home!"

We've seen this happen in the Computer Education Center at the mission. The first thing you have to teach people is that they can learn. Once they know that, their whole attitude changes and they become tremendously motivated. In the same way, once they begin to hope in Christ and to believe that with the help of God they can get a job, hold onto it, have a nice place to live, maybe someday buy a car, and even get married or get back together with their family and support their kids — then watch out!

If homeless people have no desire to better their circumstances, they are by definition mentally ill, and still deserve our compassion. I'm not talking here about the

thugs and predators who live on the street in order to prey
on other street people. There are bad guys on the streets
just like there are bad guys in every community. But the
ordinary street people want a different kind of life.

Homeless from the Start

Once I met a woman named Mandy who worked in a
clinic in Venice, California. Mandy was married and had a
two-year-old daughter. One night their house burned to
the ground. They lost everything, escaping only with what
they were wearing. Countless people offered to help them
after the fire, and Mandy told me that one of her primary
problems was finding something for all of them to do.

Mandy and her husband weren't really homeless.
They didn't spend one night out on the street. The day
after the fire they were in a furnished apartment with
clothes in the closets and food in the refrigerator. But they
had lost their business records, their mementos, their
family photo albums, their furniture — including the first
piece they had bought when they were married. Except
for one another, they had lost everything that had given
them a sense of connectedness, a sense of history and
identity as a family. Mandy told how much more difficult
daily life became after the fire, because of her sense of loss.
The simplest things, like getting her driver's license
renewed, seemed overwhelming. She felt she lacked the
capacity to do even basic tasks. Mandy estimated that this
initial disconnectedness caused her to function at only
fifty percent of her capacity to function before the fire.
Two months later she said her capacity had increased to
about eighty percent.

Mandy understood a little bit of what it meant to be

homeless. Whatever a person had before, half of it is lost the day he hits the street, simply because there is no place to live. All sense of belonging is shattered, as well as self-esteem and identity.

I asked Mandy, "Would you say homeless people are homeless because they are mentally ill, or are mentally ill because they are homeless?"

She paused a couple of minutes, giving the question a lot of thought, then said, "George, if home is a place where you belong to other people, then perhaps these people have always been homeless." I understood from her answer that if my family, the Caywoods, fell on hard times and had to live in a tent in a park, at least we would be in it together. As a unit we would handle and manage the trauma. If *home* means that sense of being related in a permanent way to people who are committed to you and care about you, then most people on skid row have always been homeless. They may have lived inside four walls from time to time, but they have never had a home.

Wounded Children

Frequently people who become homeless have been damaged early in their lives. Having been wounded as children, their capacity to function normally is already minimal, and is reduced even further when they come to the street.

I've talked to a number of psychologists about this. They compare what happens in a person's personality when he lives on the street to what has been seen in combat veterans. It's called Post-Traumatic Stress Disorder. The same type of personality destruction that happened to soldiers who fought in Vietnam happens to street people.

There is an apparently irrefutable logic operating in the minds of the homeless: *If I were worthwhile I would have something to eat. Since I have nothing to eat I cannot be worthwhile. If I were worth something I would have a place to live. I don't have a place to live, therefore I must be the scum of the earth.* This damages people profoundly. As they experience the anxiety and the fear and the horror of being on the street, their capacity to hope is drastically diminished.

Three of my daughters, Gina, Jill, and JoAnna, work in the mission's youth ministry called Kid's Club. It's not commonly known, but about one thousand children live in the hotels downtown, playing among the rats, the cockroaches, the pimps, and the pushers. The mission tries to reach these kids and my girls go downtown on Sundays to work with them.

The girls especially fell in love with one little boy who one day was hit by a van while playing in the street in front of his hotel. He ended up in a large public hospital in the area. The girls went to see him and take him some toys. In the hospital they found a number of children who had been abandoned there by their parents. Apparently this is not unusual. When a child from an impoverished home goes into the hospital, the parents assume the hospital will take care of him. A child may be there for several weeks or months and get only one or two visits from his family.

My daughters saw how frequently this happened, and it hurt them. They decided to visit some of these children. They went from room to room trying to cheer them up. Gina walked into one room, darkened in the middle of the day, and saw a fifteen-month-old baby lying in bed. God only knows what kind of abuse led to his having been hospitalized for several months. Gina walked into the room calmly and slowly as he turned his head and looked at her with huge, terrified eyes, appearing to be scared senseless.

I asked her, "Gina, why didn't he cry?"

She said, "Dad, he was way beyond crying. He quit crying weeks ago." She said the baby spoke through his eyes, saying, *I don't see any reason in the world to trust anyone, anytime, anywhere.* Gina walked over and quietly began to sing, rubbing his tummy, just loving him. She stayed with him for ten or fifteen minutes until he calmed down.

The plight of these hospitalized children seemed so heartbreaking the girls decided to go back every day. On the second day they took presents for this little boy and tried to befriend him. He relaxed a little more. On the third day he relaxed a little more. He had a little confidence, and was willing to put a little trust in them. On the fourth day he was almost like a normal little boy. When they came back on the fifth day he was gone. God only knows the circumstances he was in at that point. God only knows how long it would be before he was back in the hospital once more.

I said to Gina, "Add twenty-five years to his life. Where will he be?"

She answered, "He'll either be dead or in jail or in the Rescue Mission."

"That's right," I said. Except for what the grace of God can do, this boy may have been ruined for life before he could learn to talk. We estimate that seventy or eighty percent of the young men we work with at the mission have been sexually abused.

"Gina," I said, "imagine that little boy as a young man sitting in the chapel of the Rescue Mission, and someone from the community, inexperienced, comes in and sees him sitting there."

"Yeah," she said, "he will probably say to himself, *Why doesn't this lazy guy get a job?*"

'Do Not Judge'

It's a mistake to deal judgmentally with the poor. We must act with grace. In fact, Jesus teaches us to help even if the person in need is our enemy.

> "You have heard that it was said, 'Love your neighbor and hate your enemy.' But I tell you: Love your enemies and pray for those who persecute you, that you may be sons of your Father in heaven. He causes his sun to rise on the evil and the good, and sends rain on the righteous and the unrighteous. If you love those who love you, what reward will you get? Are not even the tax collectors doing that? And if you greet only your brothers, what are you doing more than others? Do not even pagans do that? Be perfect, therefore, as your heavenly Father is perfect." (Matthew 5:43-48)

If we are to love our enemies in this way, and to love people in need, we must first experience for ourselves that love from the Father. How many times have I asked God to turn the other cheek to me, and He has? How many times have I asked Him to go an extra mile and He has gone two? How many times have I asked Him for a small gift and He has given me a large one? How many times have I fought Him as an enemy and He showed mercy to me?

In the Luke version of this text (Luke 6:32-36), Jesus

says "Be merciful just as your Father is merciful." He is saying, *When you enter into the presence of God, and you live daily with God, you will discover that God treats you with mercy.* If we are to live according to Jesus' will, we have to know God as a giving, merciful Father. To live according to the standards Jesus Christ has given us and not be destroyed by some kind of legalism requires that we spend sufficient time in the presence of God. By experiencing God's willingness to bless us when we don't deserve it, we will be able to bless others when they don't deserve it.

God is kind to the wicked. How do I know that? Because I am wicked and God is kind to me. As I experience the kindness and mercy of God day in and day out, I am able to love my enemies. When someone asks for my shirt, I will want to give him my coat, too.

Jesus makes a logical progression. If you love people you do good to them. It means you are going to have to part with some of your money. It's going to be expensive. That, of course, is the point of the parable of the good Samaritan. To love our enemies will mean helping the homeless. Our love will inevitably lead us to do good works for people, and that will inevitably touch our checkbooks.

After telling us to be merciful as God is merciful, Jesus adds, "Do not judge" (Luke 6:37) The context of Christ's teaching here tells us to love people, to do good to people, to bless them with our money, and to not judge them. Jesus is saying, *When you love people and do good it begins to cost you money, but don't judge them. Don't use your condemnation of them as an excuse for not giving. Simply act on the basis of God's action to you.*

STAYING VULNERABLE FOR THE SAKE OF MINISTRY

MANY PEOPLE tell me their horror stories about fruitless attempts to help the homeless because they want sympathy, or want to challenge me since I've asked them to help the poor. They don't know I have lots of my own horror stories to tell.

Some of these involve panhandlers. I know how it feels to be ripped off by someone who is only pretending to have a legitimate need.

When I first began working at the mission, a man came in looking just terrible. He said he needed to go to the hospital and gave me his doctor's phone number. I called his doctor and described the symptoms the man had complained of as well as my own observations. The doctor asked me to get him to the hospital as soon as possible. I thought first of driving him there myself, but I didn't have my car and all the mission trucks were out at the time. I had only fifty cents in my pocket, not enough money for a cab. I was running around trying unsuccessfully to put together cab fare while the man was looking more ill by the minute.

Finally I gave up and said, "Look, you know I feel awful about this, but all I can do is give you bus fare. I'm terribly sorry, but I've had you sitting around here for almost an hour anyway. At least you'll be on your way to the hospital in a few minutes." He took the money, thanked me, and managed to get out the door. I felt badly about sending him off like that.

A few minutes later one of the staff people came to me and said, "You know that guy you gave bus fare to? I just saw him walking down the street twirling his cane like a dancer and acting very chipper."

The other day I heard of someone who earned as much as eight hundred dollars a day panhandling in downtown Los Angeles (he commuted from Beverly Hills). I'm not sure if I believe the story or not, but I know there is usually confusion and pain involved with the question of how to deal with panhandlers. Let me share some principles I've learned.

An Enjoyable Investment

First, if you are approached by a panhandler, you must see him as an investment opportunity. If you give him two dollars, that amount may accrue to your heavenly account as two thousand dollars. It is sometimes fun to beat a panhandler to the punch and say, "Hey, I'd like to give you a couple of dollars!" (Sometimes when a waitress approaches my table in a restaurant I say, "Hi, my name is George and I'm going to be your customer." I like to meet panhandlers in that same spirit.) The goal is to enjoy these situations and make them a positive experience.

If you are always on your guard, you see the contents of your wallet as something to be protected against a grave threat. Giving will not be a pleasant experience, when in fact it should be met as a marvelous investment opportunity. If I could persuade you to bring me some money a week from today so I could invest it for you in IBM stock at 1948 prices, you would go out and raise as much money as possible to make this high-quality investment. The panhandler may represent just such an investment opportunity for you. There is no need to see him as a threat.

Keep It Personal

Another principle I follow is to deal with the panhandler personally. I avoid any situation where I am forced to be impersonal as I attempt to help an individual. In the mind of the recipient, impersonal charity amounts to welfare, though it may have been given in the love of God. It is always important to deal with a human being as a unique personality. He is not just a homeless person. He is a human being with intellect and personality. His personhood is worth discovering and it will enrich my life, a truth that normally escapes big city planners and those who provide institutional help for the needy.

A few years ago I testified before a government commission about what the city could do in helping the homeless. They asked me to be there at 8:30 A.M. and I agreed. The previous night I didn't leave work until ten o'clock, so I was tired when I arrived on time for the commission meeting. But only the janitor was there to meet me. He offered me a cup of coffee. About ten minutes after the time I was supposed to begin testifying, the first government official appeared. Five minutes later another came, and after another half hour, six or seven of the twelve commission members had arrived. One of them finally said, "I guess we can get started now."

I started telling them what was on my heart, eventually saying, "I was at the mission until ten o'clock last night and I am very tired this morning. I was kept cooling my heels forty-five minutes until you people decided to get here. I find that humiliating. It makes me feel like you have contempt for me and my time. I don't like it. It makes me angry.

"Now, if a person like me, who has a secure home, the love of family, a good education, a good job, and a good career with a good future feels humiliated at the hands of government bureaucrats — because you've kept me waiting so long — how about a homeless person who has nothing going for him and whose self-image has already been destroyed? When you set out to help him you do it in the typical, impersonal governmental fashion, keeping him waiting around four or five hours and experiencing all that humiliation, and then you give him a place to stay. In the morning he may have had a place to sleep, but if his basic problem is low self-esteem, and you have humiliated him in the process of giving him a place to sleep, is he better off or worse off for having been helped by you?"

Offer Respect

If I decide *not* to give someone money, I thank the person anyway for the opportunity. I want him to know I respect him as a human being and appreciate the chance to talk to him and invest in eternity through him. Jesus Christ left heaven to deal with us at a very personal level, and as we turn to the world, we ought to do our best to deal personally with a person in need. Street life is very lonely. If you treat a street person with respect you will have given him something valuable even if you don't give him money.

A friend of mine, who had lived years on the street and now is doing extremely well as an employee of the mission, says the process of becoming a street person involves answering a few basic questions. First, is it possible to survive? The threat of disease and illness is terrifying. You can't stay clean, you may be mugged, you may die of hypothermia due to exposure.

After a few days of observing that other street people are surviving, you ask the second question: Can *I* survive? Street people feel like failures. They are very apt to say, *That guy is able to make it, but he's better than me or smarter than me or stronger than me. He might be able to survive, but I can't. I know how awful a person I am and how weak I am.*

A few more days go by and you realize you *are* surviving. The third question becomes the permanent question: *How* will I survive?

This question has to be answered dozens of times every day. Friendship is usually a luxury street people cannot afford; other people must be seen not as separate individuals, but as potential resources to help you survive.

I was once eating in a restaurant in San Diego, and saw out the window a guy I knew named Don. He had been on the program at the mission several years before and I really wanted to talk to him. I excused myself and I went across the street. "Hi, George," he said. He was clean and looked good, and seemed happy to see me. Less than a minute into the conversation he added, "George, can you give me two dollars?"

I was crushed. I just wanted to be his friend. Suddenly I realized that he was glad to see me primarily because he thought I could give him some money. That made me feel awful. But as I thought about it, I recognized that in living so close to the edge of survival, he did not have the luxury of just enjoying me. He needed to be able to use me. I was still free to choose how I would respond to him, however. I could act in love and with grace toward him because God always treats me in a way that builds my dignity.

Walk in the Spirit

Another principle to follow is to deal with the situation in the presence of the Holy Spirit — in the same way a Christian ought to face all of life. In any given situation, it is appropriate to ask God to help you know what to do, including how to respond to a panhandler.

Sometimes I feel strongly led to give someone money, so I act on it. At other times the Holy Spirit does not tell me what to do, but tells me what questions I ought to ask. He helps me better understand the situation. That's important to me because I don't like being lied to.

One of the implications of dealing with a panhandler in the power and wisdom of the Holy Spirit is that it calls you to honesty. It is frequently easier to say, "I can't help you," when you mean, "I won't help you." If you say "I can't help you" when you could help, you have told a lie and you are out of the Spirit. If the panhandler is also dishonest, you have entered his game on his terms; I guarantee you he is smarter at it, and he will win. Whether or not you give him money, you'll end up feeling miserable. So be careful to look a person straight in the eye and respond honestly.

Similarly, don't let a street person make you feel condemned. If condemnation takes over your thinking, you cannot be led by the Spirit. In order to survive, many street people become extremely skilled in the technique of making other people feel condemned. They've practiced for years and know exactly what to say to a Christian to make him feel guilty enough to respond. If you accept that condemnation, you are again on the panhandler's level, and you're going to lose every time. You'll feel ripped off if you give, and guilty if you don't. By rejecting condemnation and following the Spirit's guidance, you'll come out feeling comfortable because you obeyed God.

Where Your Responsibility Ends

If you do give, you are not responsible for what the panhandler does with the money. You're responsible only for your own behavior and response. If you think there's a distinct possibility the panhandler would spend your money on booze, you can invite him into a mission, or you can take him to a restaurant or grocery store and buy him food. But ultimately, if you have been obedient to God in giving to him, what he does with the money is up to him. If he abuses it, that really is his problem, and you don't need to feel bad about it.

The simple fact is, if you lose vulnerability you also lose your chance to minister. If you have come to the point where no one can take advantage of you, you have come to the point where you can't be of use to anyone. To remain vulnerable is a hard lesson to learn.

An alcoholic named Bill lived on the streets during my first years at the mission. He came to our program for three weeks. Everyone was amazed he stayed sober.

Then one Sunday morning I found him drunk. I called him into my office and asked, "Bill, what happened? Why did you start drinking?"

He said, "George, I never quit drinking."

I was devastated. I felt so ripped-off and taken advantage of. I finally got him out of my office, closed the door, and began praying. The Spirit of God helped me see that I was at the mission to be taken advantage of. To this day, that's the reason I'm here.

Some street people come to the mission to find a place to eat and a place to rest. When they leave the mission, that is all they have gotten out of it. Other people come to take advantage of the opportunity to change their lives. When they leave, they are changed. Still other people come with a desire to take advantage of what I have learned about Scripture. When they leave, they understand the Bible better. I am there for the sake of these people. If my time and money is abused, it is not my problem. I don't need to defend myself or the mission in order to minister. Because I am doing my best to be obedient to God, I can afford to remain vulnerable and soft-hearted. No one can snatch from me what I offer cheerfully out of love for God.

I've often talked about the principles in this chapter because I'm so frequently asked questions about panhandlers. I've always wondered why my remarks seem to be so poorly received. This is not abstract advice. This is what I live by. These principles are tried and true, and when I obey them I come out of the situation a winner, whether or not I give a person money.

I believe my advice is received poorly because it's a risky thing to ask for God's guidance when someone in desperate need asks you for money. What would happen if He answered, *Give them one hundred dollars,* or, *Put them up for a few nights in a hotel, as the good Samaritan did?* I find that many people prefer coming out of an exchange with a panhandler feeling miserable rather than seeking the will of God in the situation, obeying, and possibly handing over some of their money.

You can never predict the response of the Holy Spirit to a request for guidance. Jesus' standards and requirements are high. Therefore, dealing in the peace of God with a panhandler requires a commitment to do God's will at any price.

FREEDOM
IN HIS PRESENCE

FREEDOM from the love of money is based on the appreciation of two premises: God is always with me, and God is my helper. I don't have to be afraid of anything. On the basis of God's faithfulness I can let go of the love of money and live freely, because I know God will take care of me. I do not have to depend on wealth to provide for my needs.

Something for Security

If my attitude at the heart level is, *God might abandon me, God's help is unreliable* — I will feel a desperate need to accumulate cash to insulate myself against the possibility of being left high and dry, vulnerable to the fluctuations in man's economic systems. I'll feel threatened by inflation, recession, government fiscal policies, rent increases, business fluctuations, and my boss's slowness to grant the raises I need.

One of the most difficult things I have ever had to deal with has been my fear of not being able to support my family. If I were unable to take care of my wife and children, I would feel like a total failure. Therefore I've entertained a desire to be rich, to have a guarantee of being able to meet my family's needs. This fear stems from the hard time my father had in providing for his family.

How can we overcome such childhood traumas? Is it possible, based on a trust in the love of God, to abandon a need and desire for riches? Is it possible to have a relationship with God so full of confidence that I'm not tempted by the lottery, or by working endless hours to accumulate money?

The only solution given to us in Scripture is to learn to believe in the love of God. I need to have a deep belief that He will always take care of me.

My conclusion: Either I accept the love of God, and love Him in return, or I open myself to the love of money. If I'm building a love relationship with God, my love of money will decrease. If my love for God is waning, my love of money will increase. Love of money responds inversely to love of God.

Simply put, we must have something in our lives to give us security. If we do not build our hope in God, we're going to hope in money. Freeing ourselves from the love of money requires a love relationship with God.

A Reason for Confidence

The book of Hebrews encourages us to learn to live in God's loving presence.

Let us then approach the throne of grace with confidence, so that we may receive mercy and find grace to help us in our time of need...Therefore, brothers, since

we have confidence to enter the Most Holy Place by
the blood of Jesus, by a new and living way opened for
us through the curtain, that is, his body, and since we
have a great priest over the house of God, let us draw
near to God with a sincere heart in full assurance of
faith. (Hebrews 4:16,19-22)

For most of my life I maintained a wrong understanding of these verses. I believed I could come to God when I
was in trouble, find His mercy, and stay with Him to
receive His help, saying something like, *Now, God, what
did I do wrong that caused me to fall into sin? How can I prevent doing that again?* I would receive instruction, then
leave the presence of God and go about my business
knowing that if I ever need to again enter His presence,
He would be there for me.

There is something true about God being willing to
give us mercy when we sin, and to teach us how to live a
life free from sin. But He is not offering us a place to run
to only when we are in trouble. He is offering us a place to
live on a permanent, moment-by-moment basis. He
invites us to live continually in His presence.

Paul says the same thing this way: "Be joyful always;
pray continually; give thanks in all circumstances, for this
is God's will for you in Christ Jesus" (1 Thessalonians
5:16-18). It is important to hear those last three words, "in
Christ Jesus." We are invited to live *in* Christ continually,
all day, every day, and always joyfully. If we are living in
Him, we pray continually, giving thanks in all circumstances — even in an inflationary spiral or a depression,
even if we have lost a job. Our security and peace are
based on His love. Circumstances go up and down, things
go right, go wrong, are difficult, are easy. But no matter

how things are going we can still be filled with joy. We can give thanks because we are locked into the love of God, independent of circumstances.

Into His Presence

In the Old Testament, God's people were given the Tabernacle as a place to meet God. Deep inside the Tabernacle was a room where the most sacred objects were kept. In this Holy of Holies were the Ark of the Covenant, Aaron's Rod, and the Tablets of Stone containing the Ten Commandments. Once, when the Ark of the Covenant was being transported, one man thought it was going to fall, reached out his hand to steady it, and died instantly. He transgressed the awesome holiness of God because he was not authorized to touch the Ark. The Holy of Holies was the most sacred place in the world and the most fearsome place to be because it was the place God met man. Only a select few were allowed to enter.

Before the Tabernacle was built, God looked down and selected from all the people of the world a man named Abraham. From Abraham He created a nation of twelve tribes. God selected one particular tribe out of the twelve, the tribe of Levi, and from that tribe He selected one family, the family of Aaron. Aaron's family became God's priests, and out of the priests He selected one High Priest.

Once a year the High Priest went into the Holy of Holies with a rope tied around his ankle and bells on the hem of his garment. If the bells stopped jingling, people would know something had gone wrong. If he died in the Holy of Holies they could pull him out by the rope, for no one else was invited into the presence of God. Any infraction of this law resulted in death.

The Holy of Holies and the structure surrounding it — first the Tabernacle, and later the Temple — was the heart of the Jewish nation. It represented safety, the ultimate place of sanctuary. It was the seat of power and the place of worship. It was the Lincoln Monument, the White House, Arlington National Cemetery, and the Pentagon all in one. The sacred feelings and sense of history of every Jew was in that place. Only once each year a Jewish adult male of the tribe of Levi and the family of Aaron was selected from among the priests to go in. It was an awesome privilege. It was a greater honor than playing starting quarterback in the Super Bowl, or pitching the final strike-out to win the World Series!

If you are a Christian you have been selected for entrance into the Holy of Holies. You have been invited to enter not just once a year, but every day, to live there all day. Ever since Jesus Christ was crucified, rose from the dead, and ascended into heaven, He has been at that holy place where God meets man. Jesus is the Tabernacle into which the writer of Hebrews says we are to enter boldly. In Jesus Christ we experience the presence of God every day of our lives. The content of the book of Hebrews is built on this idea. We have been invited to run to God not only when we are in trouble; we have been invited to live in His presence always.

The longer and more consistently we have walked with him, the more confident we will be of His help. Confidence built through years of intimacy with God allows us to lay down our love of money. This possibility is opened to us not just because we encounter His presence in morning devotions, but because we live in His presence all day.

The writer of Hebrews makes a powerful argument for the superiority of the New Testament over the Old, because, while the Old asks for obedience to the law, the New invites us on a personal, everlasting walk with God as a result of the work Christ did on the cross. In Hebrews 1, Jesus is presented as God. In Hebrews 2, He is presented as man, our brother. Jesus was fully God and fully man and lived and died in this world. He is our salvation. Our salvation does not come by way of obedience to the law, but by way of a person to whom we are related.

> We must pay more careful attention, therefore, to what we have heard, so that we do not drift away. For if the message spoken by angels was binding, and every violation and disobedience received its just punishment, how shall we escape if we ignore such a great salvation? (2:1-3)

The writer of Hebrews does not ask, "How can we escape if we break the *laws* of this great salvation?" The issue is not breaking the law. The issue is whether or not we are going to pay attention to Christ and live in the presence of God. When we no longer ignore God, we enter into His rest.

> For anyone who enters God's rest also rests from his own work, just as God did from his. Let us, therefore, make every effort to enter that rest, so that no one will fall by following their example of disobedience. (4:10-11)

The writer of Hebrews is not telling us to make an effort to resist sin, but to make an effort to live in God's presence. It is less a question of staying on the porch saying, *I won't overeat, I won't be lustful,* and more a question of settling down in God's living room and resting.

The holy place has been opened up to us. We don't have to earn our way in. We don't have to justify our right to be there by our obedience. We come into the presence of God, and rest. When we rest in Him, obedience follows.

Real Therapy

The anxieties of our lives and our sense of inferiority are the powers that drive us to sin. God says, *Make every effort to put all that behind you, come boldly into My presence, live in My presence in full rest, and I'll teach you not to sin.* Don't let your sense of sin keep you away. God invites you, even though He knows the truth about you:

> The word of God is living and active. Sharper than any double-edged sword, it penetrates even to dividing soul and spirit, joints and marrow; it judges the thoughts and attitudes of the heart. Nothing in all creation is hidden from God's sight. Everything is uncovered and laid bare before the eyes of him to whom we must give account. (Hebrews 4:12-13)

Perhaps this sounds threatening to you — all your secret fears and sins exposed in the presence of God. Christ as the Great High Priest has fully dealt with all your sins. You therefore enter into the presence of an unthreatening God, into a rejoicing, happy rest as His child. Then God, through His Word, begins to speak deeply to your heart, cutting away, as a master surgeon, those things that bring distress. He looks deeply into your heart, penetrating the anxieties of childhood that are keeping you from enjoying peace. He uses the knife of the Word to teach you new attitudes and to separate you from those attitudes based on your own failures or the failures of your parents or the failures of people around you. He gives you attitudes based on the impossibility that God the Father would ever fail you.

I am talking about real therapy here, real psycho-therapy, fully backed by the comfort and love of God, and including courage to face attitudes that keep you sinning. This is, of course, an exact reversal of what we expect. The Old Testament pattern says, *Obey the law and therefore live in God's presence.* The New Testament contract is, *Forget about trying to be righteous on your own; live in the presence of God based on the righteousness of Jesus, and learn obedience.*

We allow God to deal with our deepest sins because we have known His love. We know the holiness of God has been fully satisfied in Jesus Christ. We are safe to be exactly who we are. We can be open with God because God has proven His love. We make ourselves vulnerable to Him because we have learned He is safe to be with, even as He begins peeling away the many layers of defense mechanisms we have erected to protect the hurting, tender places of our life.

God is a peace-maker, not just a peace-keeper. God wants to solve our deep problems, not just keep our life smooth. We don't need more of God's love, for He has given us all of it. What we need is to unload the things that interfere with the flow of God's love in our lives. We need to have confidence, based on experience, that in God's presence we can open ourselves to Him and He will remove our defenses, and we can connect with His love.

"Don't you care if we drown?" Compare these words, addressed to Jesus by the spiritually immature Peter and the other disciples during a storm at sea (Mark 4:38), with Peter's statement decades later: "Cast all your anxiety on him because he cares for you." (1 Peter 5:7). What made the difference? Years of living in the presence of God, years of risking everything for His kingdom, years of taking up a cross daily and following hard after Jesus. Those years took him from insecurity to the maturity of living above life's ups and downs, through the deep knowledge that God *does* care — profoundly.

We need to learn again the secrets of contemplation, of spending an hour meditating on Scripture, allowing God to feed our hearts. We must learn to hear from God all day, every day, as His children. I have adult children and I love sharing their lives. I don't want them to come to my house and hide in a closet. I want them to come to me when they need to cry. I want them to come and laugh with me. One of the most exciting things in my life is to get a call from one of my daughters saying, "Dad, I want to have lunch with you. I want to talk to you." God wants to be far more available to us and far more intimate with us than we are prepared to believe.

When living in God's presence becomes a lifestyle for us, we begin to learn of God's incredible love. On the basis of God's love, we are able to let go of the love of money. Many of us have been hurt and wounded and have built all kinds of barriers to love. Jesus understands the battle we are in. Jesus understands what it means to be brutalized. He wants us to become comfortable in God's love, so He can begin to break down those barriers. Our defenses will be weakened and eventually destroyed by His love.

Christ's Example

As we live in this love, Jesus is our perfect High Priest, we are told, because He is a priest forever, and is without sin:

Therefore, since we have a great high priest who has gone through the heavens, Jesus the Son of God, let us hold firmly to the faith we profess. For we do not have a high priest who is unable to sympathize with our weaknesses, but we have one who has been tempted in every way, just as we are — yet was without sin. Let us then approach the throne of grace with confidence, so that we may receive mercy and find grace to help us in our time of need. (Hebrews 4:14-16)

Jesus lives eternally, so the day will never come when the presence of God becomes unsafe for us. The writer of Hebrews tell us our salvation is not limited by time. It is eternal.

We read also in Hebrews that although Jesus was God's Son,

he learned obedience from what he suffered and, once made perfect, he became the source of eternal salvation for all who obey him and was designated by God to be high priest in the order of Melchizedek. (Hebrews 5:8-10)

It doesn't seem right that Jesus had to *learn* obedience, but He did. He learned to obey in the tough spots, through things He suffered. It is one thing to obey when the command of God makes sense. It is another thing to obey and stay steady with God when everything seems to go wrong. That's how it felt to Jesus before the crucifixion. He said, *Father, let this cup pass from Me. It seems right to Me that I don't go through this. Let it pass from Me. But I want to do Your will. I want to do what You want Me to do.*

Because He was obedient when everything in Him was crying out not to be, Jesus was made perfect and mature. His life was complete.

It is no different for us. We need suffering in this world. We don't have to seek it. It will always present itself. We can learn obedience only when life isn't making sense, when everything within us is crying out to God, "Remove this cup!" If we can remain steady, staying in the presence of God and doing what we are supposed to do, we will be brought to maturity.

A few months ago a highly placed businessman, an active supporter of our mission, became upset at some things we were doing. We needed this man's support, and it seemed to me that our ability to accomplish our goals required us to have a good relationship with him. I set up an appointment to meet with him the following week, giving me five days to anticipate our encounter.

Since I grew up in a poor home, I learned to feel intimidated by wealthy people. The thought of having to walk into this man's huge office, located high in a business tower downtown, provoked my childhood fears and threatened my self-esteem. I prayed, "Lord, I don't want to do this. Remove this from me." But, of course, God didn't do that, and I kept my appointment.

Based on my assurance of God's presence, I showed up at five o'clock that Tuesday afternoon and had an honest, heart-to-heart discussion with this wonderful man. We worked out the problem that was frustrating him and came to a solution. At five-thirty I walked out of his office as a more mature individual than I had been at five o'clock, because I had been obedient when I hadn't wanted to obey.

God puts me in situations designed by the Holy Spirit

to arouse my worst fears. As those fears are provoked, God enables me to get through the situation. I become less afraid in those areas and I move toward maturity. I have increasing confidence — based on experience, based on suffering, based on facing things that scare me. By walking through my little Gethsemanes every day, I am becoming more mature. I am becoming more complete. My joy is being made full.

The message of Hebrews is a call to live a life of obedience, to be willing to suffer, to be willing to go through whatever God allows — difficult financial times, difficult emotional times — knowing that I am in the Holy of Holies, as safe as an infant nursing at its mother's breast.

The writer of Hebrews wants to convince us this relationship with God does not depend on *our* work, but on the work of Jesus Christ. We can be secure children, safe in the embrace of One who profoundly loves us.

As I have wrestled with difficulties in my life, I've realized that I was not adequately parented, nor do I adequately parent my own children. I've learned that the only adequate parent is God Himself. The only fully nurturing parent is God. The only fully protecting Father is God. I have learned to love and respect my father and mother for what they gave me and to thank God for them, and I've stopped wishing they had been perfect parents. Because God is both the perfect Father and the perfect Mother for all of us.

I also no longer expect myself to be the perfect father, and I am encouraging my children as they become adults to turn to the Father who is perfect and complete. I turn to God for the parenting and the nurturing and the acceptance and the training I need.

As this process continues in my life, I understand that

my heavenly Father will never leave me, never forsake me. He is my Helper. It is unnecessary for me to be afraid of people or the systems of this world. In the presence of my Father I am acceptable. He loves me, His world is a safe place for me to live, and I don't have to rely on money to give me what He Himself generously provides.

A QUESTION OF THE HEART

NEW TESTAMENT CHRISTIANS were selling personal possessions and bringing money to the apostles to support the revival in Jerusalem. Caught up in the spirit of what was happening, and wanting to be part of the action, Ananias and Sapphira sold a piece of personal property and gave the money to the apostles. But they secretly kept back some of the money for themselves.

> Then Peter said, "Ananias, how is it that Satan has so filled your heart that you have lied to the Holy Spirit and you kept for yourself some of the money you received for the land? Didn't it belong to you before it was sold? And after it was sold wasn't the money at your disposal? What made you think of doing such a thing? You have not lied to men but to God." (Acts 5:3-4)

Peter frankly acknowledged that Ananias had a right to keep his property. And once it had been sold Ananias had all rights to come to Peter and say, *Here's eighty percent of the profits,* or *Here's fifty percent of the profits,* or even

Here's forty percent of the profits. The problem was that Ananias had only pretended he was committed to the level of
giving everything.

In the context of what I've gleaned from my studies in
Luke, that's a little frightening to me. For if Christians
were immediately judged today as Ananias and Sapphira
were — on the reality of their commitment as compared to
their words — there might be some real drama in the
church. As we beg for God to pour out his Holy Spirit, He
may hesitate to do so because one side of an outpouring of
the Holy Spirit is for people to be saved and healed; the
other side is the judgment of sin within the church. Perhaps God hesitates to answer when we pray for revival
because the judgment side would be so devastating.

Can a Christian Drive a BMW?

Several fine Christian leaders have spoken out against
materialism in the church and how it contradicts our pro-
fessed commitment. Some of these leaders have made
strong statements — such as a declaration that no Christian should drive a forty-thousand-dollar automobile. In
view of the number of starving people throughout the
world, their reasoning goes, the conscience of a serious
Christian should allow him to drive only a car worth ten
or twenty thousand dollars. *If Christ were here,* these leaders claim, *He would certainly opt for a cheaper car.*

Some of the people arguing for this have been to Calcutta or Haiti or other places where it is common to see
people starving. The terror of what they've seen has deep-
ened their conviction to be absolutely faithful to God and
not be dominated by a love of money.

My thinking on this matter is that Christ probably

wouldn't have driven even a ten-thousand-dollar car. He probably would have walked or used public transportation. (It's a substantial step up from poverty to drive even a very old Toyota.)

But to argue about what kind of car Christians should drive keeps the discussion of materialism at a low level, in light of the demand Christ made on some people to sell everything and give to the poor, and in light of His own example:

> Your attitude should be the same as that of Christ Jesus: Who, being in very nature God, did not consider equality with God something to be grasped, but made himself nothing… (Philippians 2:5-6)

In Luke 14:33, we are told to give up everything if we are to be His disciples. Jesus' command is to prepare ourselves to sell everything we have and give to the poor, a much more fundamental commitment than simply settling for an Escort over a BMW.

When I first read the arguments about appropriate cars for Christians, they overwhelmed me. They threw me into an endless debate over every purchase. I suppose I could get along with one suit and sell all my others. On the other hand, in directing our mission I need fresh clothes as I encounter various public officials.

It seems to me that in Scripture God always equipped His people, never hesitating to provide the tools needed to fight His wars. I don't see any indication in the accounts of Paul's journeys in Acts that he had any trouble raising ship fares. He seemed able to travel as he needed to. I agree that we should restrict purchases to create disposable income for giving. I agree I need to be reminded to handle money wisely. But the sense of judgment in the statement about what cars we should drive does not help me repent. It hinders me as I try to repent.

As I wrestle with my responsibility toward the poor I feel conflict between the needs of my ministry and family and the needs of the poor. Scripture acknowledges that having a family limits one's ability to commit to Christ. In Paul's view there are real advantages to being single.

> I would like you to be free from concern. An unmarried man is concerned about the Lord's affairs — how he can please the Lord. But a married man is concerned about the affairs of this world — how he can please his wife — and his interests are divided. An unmarried woman or virgin is concerned about the Lord's affairs: Her aim is to be devoted to the Lord in both body and spirit. But a married woman is concerned about the affairs of this world — how she can please her husband. I am saying this for your own good, not to restrict you, but that you may live in a right way in undivided devotion to the Lord. (1 Corinthians 7:32-25)

Paul says if a person is married, it imposes a limit on the freedom with which he can serve the Lord. If you add a number of children (in my case, four) to that formula, it naturally restricts the freedom to do things like selling everything you have and giving to the poor. The reason, Paul indicates, is that certain things are expected of a married man. Being a good father, helping my children get the education they need, and providing food and a secure place for them to live are all a fulfillment of my responsibility before God.

Time to Grow

Yet beyond the limits of family and ministry I see a need
for a deeper commitment — and time to grow into it. To
make a blanket statement about what kind of car to drive
or how much to give, and to impose this on all Christians,
does not acknowledge the growth process. God's way is to
meet us where we are and to lead us into an ever deeper
commitment.

If today I sold all I had and gave it to the poor, it
wouldn't do me much good as a disciple because it would
be done grudgingly. Scripture teaches us that God loves a
cheerful giver. I need time to learn to give with joy. As I
understand what has been given to me by God I can give
more cheerfully. We can lead each other through a growth
process where we start to imitate each other and begin to
outgive each other. Listen again to Paul:

> I am not commanding you, but I want to test the sin-
> cerity and love by comparing it with the earnestness of
> others. For you know the grace of our Lord Jesus
> Christ, that though He was rich, yet for your sakes He
> became poor, so that you through His poverty might
> become rich. (2 Corinthians 8: 8-9)

He is telling the Corinthian Christians, *I'm not com-
manding you to give sacrificially, I'm simply inviting you to
test the level of your sincerity against the standard of the generosity of Jesus Christ, who left everything for our sake that we
might have everything.* Paul observes that the extent to
which we have learned the grace of God is the extent to
which we have learned to be gracious. If our level of
giving is relatively low, it is because we have not clearly
seen the grace of God in His giving to us.

A test is designed to show where you need work and improvement. When I test myself, I can see areas where I need to grow and improve. When I've repented in those areas, I don't relax and go about my business; I take another progress test. I compare myself again to the loving and giving example of Jesus Christ, and I say, *Well, here are a few more areas in which I need to improve.*

By constantly comparing ourselves to the grace and mercy of God, we receive an increasingly penetrating view of His love. The apostle John says, "We love because he first loved us" (1 John 4:19). I look at Christ, and my encounter with His grace enables me to turn from Him to you, and to love you generously and practically in ways that cover you in your hour of need.

Those who don't own a car will tend to find an excuse not to be generous when acceptable commitment to the gospel is based on how expensive a person's car is. But when it comes to giving, no one is excused. It is not a question of amount, but of the heart. We are all asked to give according to our ability.

> For if the willingness is there, the gift is acceptable according to what one has, not according to what he does not have. (2 Corinthians 8:12)

In God's eyes it may be just as wonderful for one person to give up his ten-speed bicycle for a three-speed, as for someone else to give up a BMW for a Toyota — because giving must always be a matter of the heart. We are not judged by what we don't have but by what we do have.

Again, giving for Christians must be joyful. To read statements like "Christians shouldn't drive expensive cars," does not engender in me a spirit of the joy of giving.

It makes me feel condemned. It makes giving a duty for me instead of a privilege — the kind of privilege Paul described.

> And now, brothers, we want you to know about the grace that God has given the Macedonian churches. Out of the most severe trial, their overflowing joy and their extreme poverty welled up in rich generosity. For I testify that they gave as much as they were able, and even beyond their ability. Entirely on their own, they urgently pleaded with us for the privilege of sharing in this service to the saints. (2 Corinthians 8:1-4)

The generosity of these churches prompted Paul to say, *No, I won't take this money. You're giving too deeply.* And they said, *O Paul, please let us give. We want to so badly.* If we desire to see the body of Christ practice real generosity as a lifestyle we must teach the joy of giving from a heart persuaded by the love of God. And we must teach people to give out of an enlightened self-interest, because giving is a good investment for them.

The Wrong Sorrow

Statements that condemn are counter-productive. They produce the act they are intended to prevent. Paul says in 2 Corinthians 7:10, "Godly sorrow brings repentance that leads to salvation and leaves no regret. But worldly sorrow brings death." What's the difference between the sorrow that brings repentance and the sorrow that brings death? Godly sorrow is based on conviction, whereas worldly sorrow is based on condemnation. Conviction is from God; condemnation is not.

Conviction is by its nature *particular*. When God convicts me He says to me, *Yesterday afternoon, at two o'clock, when that man asked you for money, you didn't give it to him, and I wanted you to.* That's conviction. In response I say, *O dear Lord, I am sorry. If I can find him, I'll give him the money, and in the future I'll try to be more sensitive because I really want to be like You.* That's the healthy and godly sorrow that leads to repentance.

Conviction has to do with specific events that happened in a specific time and place. Condemnation has to do with me and my nature. Ungodly sorrow is when I turn conviction to condemnation, saying, *Since I did not give money to that person yesterday afternoon at two o'clock, I must not be a real Christian. I'm no good.* If I feel I'm no good, I'll behave in a way that is no good.

If I continually told my daughter, Janelle, who is a kind and generous person, *You are a rotten liar,* in a matter of time she would become a rotten liar. Condemnation defeats and leads to death, whereas conviction is godly and leads to repentance.

Riches to Enjoy

I see a pattern in which God has used the kindhearted wealthy to benefit the poor. As we saw earlier, the rich man in the parable of Lazarus was judged because he didn't meet the needs of the man on his doorstep. Cornelius and the centurion did not sell *everything*, but they were not rebuked; they were praised and rewarded because they gave a portion of what they had — to the temple in one case, and to the poor in the other. It is not wrong to be wealthy. It is wrong to be self-centered.

One of my daughters was grieving once over a dress

she had bought. She wondered if she had been wrong to buy it since there is so much need in the world. I read her this passage from Scripture:

> Command those who are rich in this present world not to be arrogant nor to put their hope in wealth which is so uncertain, but to put their hope in God, who richly provides us with everything for our enjoyment. Command them to do good, to be rich in good deeds, and to be generous and willing to share. In this way they will lay up treasure for themselves as a firm foundation for the coming age, so that they may take hold of the life that is truly life. (1 Timothy 6:17-19)

I asked her, "Why did God give you the resources to buy that dress?"

She answered, "So I could help the poor." Her answer was predictable, but not scriptural. I pointed her back to 1 Timothy 6:17. Then she noticed God had given her all things for her enjoyment. She was astounded. This passage teaches us that God wants us to enjoy what He gives us. But two things will ruin the party: First, if we trust in our resources instead of in Him. Second, if we allow our possessions to make us arrogant, self-indulgent, and free to ignore the needs of others.

A Bigger Kingdom

The overall goal for the body of Christ is that we all live equally well, as Paul explains.

> Our desire is not that others might be relieved while you are hard pressed, but that there might be equality.

At the present time your plenty will supply what they need, so that in turn their plenty will supply what you need. Then there will be equality, as it is written: "He that gathered much did not have too much, and he that gathered little did not have too little." (2 Corinthians 8: 13-15)

It is one thing for us to say the kingdom of God is the United States of America, and to set a goal that all Christians in America will live equally well. But the kingdom of God does not respect national boundaries. The kingdom of God is bigger than the Jewish nation, and the kingdom of God is certainly bigger than the American nation. When we consider equality in terms of financial privilege in the world, as we are instructed to do in 2 Corinthians 8, we have to consider the desperate situation of our brothers throughout the world.

Paul's purpose is not to strip us in order to make others rich. He is saying God has trusted some of His people with more than they need in order to help others who have less than they need. I think this principle of equality should influence the kind of cars we drive and the kind of immigration laws we support.

There is justice in the statement that no Christian should drive a forty-thousand-dollar car. It is, at heart, however, a legalistic statement. The law has not, does not, and *will* not produce righteousness. Transformation through God's love is the reality that will move us toward a joyful willingness to sell all and give to the poor.

MINISTRY CREATES UNITY

AFTER WORKING with skid row children at the mission's Kid's Club one day, one of my daughters came home discouraged.

"Dad," she asked, "why won't the people in the churches do more?"

"What do you mean?" I questioned.

"Well, if the people in the churches would help, we could do so much more for these kids."

One critical reason the church does not do more is the lack in the twentieth-century American church of the fundamental unity so apparent in the book of Acts. Without unity, we have little to offer the world.

Jesus said, "All men will know that you are my disciples if you love one another" (John 13:35). And Jesus prayed, "...that all of them may be one, Father, just as you are in me and I am in you. May they also be in us so that the world may believe that you have sent me" (John 17:21). Jesus is describing something potentially very powerful, because He asks God to unify you and me to the same extent that He is unified with His Father.

By our love the world shall know we belong to Jesus Christ. And by our unity the world becomes persuaded that Jesus is from the Father. If we do not love each other, the world will not believe we are His disciples. If we are not one, the world will not believe Jesus is God's Son.

No Ammunition

Picture this: A group of military commanders are sitting around a table planning their strategy for an upcoming battle. The Air Force commander argues eloquently for launching the main attack by air. The Navy admiral says it should come by sea. The Army general says an opening assault from his ground forces would be the most effective blow. And the Marine commander declares that his troops are the toughest and should be allowed to lead the attack wherever it occurs.

The arguments fly around the table. A younger official, fresh from the Pentagon, sits at one end. He listens for a while, then says, "Wait a minute, stop arguing. There's no ammunition for anyone."

That's the condition of the American church today. We can make strategies about how best to reach the world with the love of God, we can argue various theological points of view, but we are firing empty guns if we don't love each other and aren't unified. We'll fail to persuade the world that Jesus is from the Father, and we'll fail to persuade the world that Christ can bring them into a saving relationship with God.

Many years ago the staff at one of our mission facilities was in a struggle with the staff of a neighboring mission facility. There was a lot of jealousy between the two. I talked with one of the directors, trying to describe the power of love and unity to draw outsiders and unsaved to the program. He said to me, "You know George, love frightens people."

I could understand that. A group of people on Main Street are firmly convinced I am a homosexual because I've tried to love people. They've never experienced Christian love, so they interpret my actions according to their own patterns of behavior. If someone has never known love from a mother and father as he grew up, then when you offer him love, it is a frightening, unbelievable thing.

I shared with the director an experience my family had in moving to a new community. We tried to love our neighbors, and it frightened them, too. They thought we were weird. We decided to open the doors and windows of our house and let our neighbors see we loved each other within the family. On that basis we gained a right with some of them to share the love of God.

While the people this director was trying to reach were not able to receive love directly, if the two mission facilities would work together, if the staffs would quit bickering and start to love each other, they would create a situation comparable to a bonfire on a cold winter night. If the workers at those facilities were willing to lay down their lives for the sake of each other's ministries, those who were out in the loveless cold would be drawn inevitably toward the warmth. But the lack of unity and love in the church strips away our right to share the love of God with the world.

Work First, Growth Second, Unity Third

In his letter to the Ephesians, Paul provides the picture of what God wants His church to be.

It was he [Christ] who gave some to be apostles, some
to be prophets, some to be evangelists, and some to be
pastors and teachers, to prepare God's people for
works of service, so that the body of Christ may be
built up until we all reach unity in the faith and in the
knowledge of the Son of God and become mature,
attaining to the whole measure of the fullness of
Christ. (4:11-13)

The leadership — apostles, prophets, evangelists, pastors and teachers — are given in the biblical picture as a
gift to the church. It's as if your pastor has a ribbon
wrapped around him when he stands in the pulpit. He is a
gift to the church. As such, the task of the church leadership is first to see that God's people are prepared to work;
second, to see that the body of Christ is built up; and
third, to see that we reach unity.

We have reversed the order. We want to find unity
first, then build the body up, then go to work. We come
into a community and say, for example, "Okay, all the
Baptists over in this corner." So all the Baptists go to their
corner and then we say, "But you're American Baptist and
we're Conservative Baptist, so you don't belong in this
corner, you belong over there in the other corner." We
have reduced the body of Christ to narrow compartments
of people who agree as closely as possible to each other's
categories of thought, and function as compatibly as possible with each other's systems.

All the while we're thinking, *This is unity. See how we
love each other in this little corner!* Our next strategy is to
gradually build each other up, hoping someday we'll be
strong enough to go out into the community, win people
to Christ, and do the work of God.

But Paul tells us in Ephesians to put a new convert to work right away. In the process of being involved in the work of the church in the community, he becomes a part of the whole body of Christ.

There is a tremendous diversity of people at Union Rescue Mission, but because of the pressing nature of the needs of the poor and the common desire to bring the love of Christ to them, we are thrown together and forced to support each other. We reach out to each other despite our differences, because the demands of the work are so great.

When we begin by doing the work of God, the stress of warfare in the world creates a dependency and a concern that build up the church and make its members strong. Out of that, comes unity. That's how God makes it happen.

People are built up as they do the work; and unity is achieved in this building-up process. If we try to begin with unity, we'll never have unity; if we try to build people up before we send them into the world, they will spend all their lives sitting in the pews and the work will never get done. We do not get mature in order to serve; we serve in order to gain maturity.

Holy Service

We think we have to make people holy enough to serve God. That's because our concept of holiness is a matter of what goes on inside our hearts and minds. But in Scripture, the concept of holiness is what we do in the world; it is taking on the evil of this world and defeating it. Essentially our immature theology says, "I'll get holy (meaning I will bring the lust of the flesh under control), and then I'll serve. If I haven't brought the lust of the flesh under control, then I ought not to serve; I'm unworthy to serve."

If by *serve* we mean to be in authority, then a servant definitely does need to have control over his flesh. Our spiritual leaders must achieve victory over fleshly desires. But if by *serve* we mean simply helping people, blessing people, and consistently giving and meeting the needs of the poor, then that service ought to start from the day we become a Christian. This service will produce holiness in us. It is in the serving, in the giving, that we encounter Christ, and begin to find produced in us what it takes to find victory over our passions. In the pressure of the work of ministry God gives grace to be victorious over sin. If you are waiting to have victory over sin before you begin to serve, you will never have victory over sin.

To say a holy person is someone who has his passions under control is like saying doctors have a sixth-grade education. That certainly is true; every M.D. I've met has a sixth-grade education. But that is describing his education at such a low level it becomes almost a deception, an item of misinformation. Holy people are people who do the work of Christ as defined in Scripture, marching against the gates of Hades and attacking evil in the world, destroying the works of the devil. Certainly mature spiritual warriors and real leaders have their passions under control. But to define holiness as simply attacking the evil inside our skin and not the evil in the world is a different definition of holiness than is given in Scripture.

Holiness emphasizes *impact* on the world. The holiness of God is not something abstract happening in heaven. The holiness of God is His fierce, warlike nature driving Him to invade earth with His kingdom.

A related problem is our defining *service* as what goes on inside the church, instead of what the Christian does in the world. The range of acceptable calls to ministry has become limited to the tasks necessary to keep a church functioning. The issue is more a question of fitting people into church roles than helping people come to a radical fulfillment of all God called them to be. A person with triangular gifts is jammed into a square hole because he seems to fit better than the person with round gifts. The problem is compounded by powerful motivational preaching that calls people to serve when, in fact, there are few real avenues of service and even fewer situations where the gift matches the task. Meanwhile the world perishes.

During my time at Union Rescue Mission I've undergone a learning process regarding the relationship of the mission to the church. Early on I noticed that the only street people who prospered spiritually were those who got involved with the local church. So I got excited and began to work hard at getting them into local churches.

Problems emerged as the churches were overwhelmed by the attendance of street people who were not truly becoming part of the church's life. The expected results were not occurring. In response, we began to require people from the mission to become more active in the church's ministry and fellowship.

We began to recruit church people to come to the mission to help bridge the gap. Some outstanding relationships developed and some of the volunteers prospered for a time. But generally, the church people got chewed up like hamburger because of the tremendous stress of this ministry. Then I took on myself the responsibility to keep the volunteers encouraged, and I burned out. My ministry suffered and I became discouraged.

An Alternative Model

From this evolution in my understanding, I want to suggest an alternative model. To illustrate it I will use a church of three hundred families. In this church, about seventy-five families are on the fringe of things. Many will remain on the fringe more or less permanently, but others will ultimately leave the fringe and move toward deeper commitment.

Of the remaining families, fifty constitute the "church ministry," fifty make up the "community ministry," and the other one hundred twenty-five families are the "support ministry."

The fifty church ministry families are the ushers, the Sunday school teachers, all those who keep the church functioning. Some of the fringe families may also help out at this level.

The fifty community ministry families evangelize in hospitals, jails and missions. In particular, they lead the church in adopting formerly institutionalized people coming off the mission program. While providing emotional support and a place to live, they help them become fully integrated into the church and community.

The support ministry families support the community ministry members by meeting regularly with them, encouraging them, and helping them. *Prayer* is their first commitment. Volunteering *services* is their second commitment. Freeing up *time* for the community ministry team is a third commitment. In other words, the support ministry families pray, mow the lawns, fix the cars, and clean and paint the houses, as well as communicate encouragement and praise for the community ministry families — all for the purpose of releasing them to minister. (This way, rather than taking away hours of family time from community ministry families, we give hours back to them by allowing others to bear part of the burden of their household responsibilities and other ordinary duties. The hours sacrificed to community ministry don't have to come from family time or husband-and-wife time, but from housecleaning or lawn-mowing time.) Some fringe and church ministry families will gradually be drawn to this support ministry.

The pastors in this alternative model of the church are there not to do the work of ministry, but to see that the people do the work. When I worked for the Marriott Corporation, I managed an accounting department. As manager I wasn't expected to have an adding machine on my desk — I was not there to do the work of the department, but to see that others got it done.

In the same way, the pastor is not there to do the ministry. He is there as a facilitator, to see to it that people do the ministry. His job comes directly from Ephesians 4. He must understand the gifts and calling of his people so that when an opportunity to minister appears, he can match the available ministry with the right family who would be thrilled with the opportunity.

That means he and his staff spend a lot of time getting to know people intimately. The pastor must become an expert at delegating responsibility on the administrative level, so he is free to spend time with people, following the pattern Jesus set down with His disciples.

The People's Vision

In this model it wouldn't be important for the pastor to have his own vision for the church. What matters is not his vision, but the vision of the people. The most reasonable way to determine the work God has for a church is to understand the vision and calling God has placed in the hearts of its people.

If I go to a pastor and say, "I would like your church to be involved with the poor," and he answers, "Well, I already work seventy hours a week; you must want me to work seventy-five," then I know he himself is trying to do the work God intended one or two hundred families to do. But if he has faithfully preached the gospel and taught the Word, he has a church full of people eager to minister. His job becomes hooking up family A with ministry A, and family B with ministry B.

If the dominating vision in the church is only the pastor's vision, he must constantly find ways to motivate people to follow his vision. The easiest way to motivate people is to make them feel guilty, so he is often forced to drive people by guilt. But if he is there to help them achieve *their* dream for God, he doesn't need to find ways to motivate them. They provide their own. The pulpit exists to help people get into their own vision.

The pastor must learn to keep one eye open toward ministry families who are beginning to bog down. When that happens, he puts the resources of the church to use to overcome whatever problems have occurred. Frequently the problem is only a molehill perceived as a mountain. Beginning ministers tend to get tripped up by stones, not boulders. The pastor must become skilled at helping people remove stones and kick down molehills.

When you're trying to get a ministry started, it's not the overwhelming problems that stop you. To those, you say, "I know God is going to come through." The real hang-ups are the little things, like, "How am I going to get

this family from one part of town to another?" If the
pastor knows another family with a van who want to
serve, he says, "Don't worry, I'll talk to this family about
providing the transportation." Then the little stone bog-
ging down the process is kicked out of the way, without
the pastor having to do the work. He is simply the person
coordinating the vast resources of the local church.

The effect of this ministry pattern is that, in this fellowship of three hundred families, the church is a committee
of two hundred and ninety-nine families supporting the
work of one family's ministry. That family, in turn, is part
of another committee of two hundred and ninety-nine
families supporting another family's ministry, and so on.
The entire church is organized around the ministry of its
people.

Ministry Time, Family Time

Notice that we're not talking about *individual* ministry, but
family ministry. We must find creative ways in which families can minister together in every setting. If the father
ministers alone, the ministry becomes the enemy of the
family. If Dad, Mom, and kids minister together, the ministry becomes an asset to the family.

My entire family has been used by God on skid row.
When I listen to my kids reviewing their years growing
up, I hear about trips to Disneyland and beach vacations,
but what I hear about most are the ministry times we've
shared together, such as times we've had fifteen or twenty
street people from the mission to our home for dinner.

Ministry time is the best quality time. It's better than
anything else you can do with your children. And it is
amazing how powerfully the youngest child can minister

if given the opportunity and encouraged to do so. My
children, while well under the age of ten, were effective
ministers at Union Rescue Mission. Of course, I protected
them and drew limits for them, but within the safe context
I provided they were able to minister in a wonderful way.

Many people do not live in families, of course, and
these people should not be excluded from ministry.
Instead, they can become members of a ministry team and
thereby supplied with a "family." These teams would be
organized not on the basis of age or marital status or
neighborhood, but on the basis of a mutual call.

For example, all the people interested in child evangelism could be on either the child evangelism support team
or the child evangelism ministry team. The same for those
who want to repair the houses of widows and the poor,
and so on.

In this way every team would have representatives of
each age group. The mixture of ages would solve one of
the churches worst problems: the isolation of the young
from the old.

Young people need old people and old people need
young people. Babies need the elderly and the elderly
need babies. A ten-year-old can have a burden for the
poor if he is given the opportunity, and it's a burden he
can easily share with an eighty-year-old.

Inside or Outside?

We have to understand and accept the reality that outside
ministry is neither clean nor cool. Real ministry is always
an exhausting, messy business. The calm, laid-back atmo-
sphere in the local church would disappear in a hurry if
members were involved in ministry, because it is tiring

and tough, and yet also exciting and fulfilling. If you don't believe it, look at the life of Christ.

Churches are not functioning at optimum level because we have defined ministry as what happens inside the church. When someone gets saved we say, "Well, do you want to be an usher, teach Sunday school, or sing in the choir?" Hospital and jail visitation, getting involved in the pain of a broken family, hospitality to the poor — these are given low priority, perhaps saved for spiritual giants. We set our sights too low by not believing in the ability of the average layperson to have a burden and ability for doing community ministry.

We ought to focus first on the community, because if our focus is not on the community we are inexperienced in the gospel. And keep in mind that the gospel sharing modeled by Christ included helping the afflicted and was not limited to preaching the plan of salvation.

Unashamed of the Gospel

Paul said,

> I am not ashamed of the gospel, because it is the power of God for salvation of everyone who believes: first for the Jew, then for the Gentile. (Romans 1:16)

Why wasn't Paul ashamed of the gospel? Why was he willing to go out into the world with the love of God? Because he knew the gospel is the power of God to bring salvation. How did he know that? Because he'd been so thoroughly changed himself and had seen hundreds of other people changed through a powerful ministry.

Let's say you had cancer and I had a cure, some new

drug that would totally drive cancer from your body. I
knew it worked because it cured *me* of cancer, and I had
seen it cure others as well. If I came to you saying, "Take
this pill, it will rid you of cancer," and you said, "Get
away from me; you always were weird," your rebuke
wouldn't stop me if I loved you. I'd argue with you. I'd do
anything to get you to take this pill. You could disdain me,
you could be angry at me, you could reject me, but it
wouldn't even slow me down if I cared about you.

We don't know the gospel is the power of God for salvation because we haven't seen the gospel in operation.
We haven't seen its power to change people, because the
focus of our ministry is on the church and not the community.

Sometimes our mission is visited by a group from a
church whose members are not at all intimidated by a
drunk laying on the sidewalk outside the front door. Why
are they not intimidated? Because about half their congregation used to be substance abusers. Two-thirds of their
deacons were once drug addicts who got saved. On a typical Sunday in their church another druggie, pale and ema-
ciated and sloppily dressed, is saved. Then week after
week, Sunday after Sunday, they see him gradually
change. In four or five years, he becomes a deacon. They
see the progress.

It's much easier to get people from this church to work
on skid row than it is to get people from other churches,
because in this church they're not ashamed of the gospel.
They've seen it work.

Churches whose people are prepared to serve see the
results Jesus predicted. They go out into the community,
and because they know service in the world is always
costly, always exhausting, they demonstrate love for one

another by supporting each other in practical ways. Other people see the love they have for each other, and no one has to try to convince them of the love of God. Power and authority is restored to the church, and the world is drawn to Jesus Christ.

NOT PERFORMANCE, BUT PERSPECTIVE

A FRIEND OF MINE asked a psychologist, "What is considered the ultimate evil?" His friend quickly answered, "The ultimate psychological evil is denial."

In certain situations, the ability to deny is essential to our mental health. We use it when we get more negative input than can be managed. When I was fifteen, for example, the ramifications of my father's death were overwhelming to me. I simply could not deal with them at the time. Most of what I had to face went into my subconscious. I was able to put it out of my thoughts. In God's plan, over the next months and years I was allowed to process some of the sense of loss and tragedy. Ideally, the mourning process will involve hauling into the conscious mind the painful thoughts and painful realities, facing them, then dealing with them over a period of one to two years. All this is perfectly normal and valuable.

However, denial can be abused when we bury in the subconscious mind anything we don't want to think about and leave it there permanently. In that case, it becomes what I have learned to call "emotional fat."

Unfortunately, for most of my life I have eaten more food than I have been able to burn off through exercise, and physical fat — unprocessed calories — has been built up. Unprocessed pain becomes emotional fat, and is destructive to the soul.

Reality — And Our Response

Though many Christians prefer to hide from the harsh situations people endure on planet earth, the first active step we all need to take as we attempt to deal with our obligation to others is to systematically face the terrible reality of the poor in our cities, our country, and our world. The reality is that thousands upon thousands of people...

> — live on the city dumps of the world.
> — will die of starvation today.
> — are being ravaged by wars perpetrated by the rich and powerful to protect their own interests, including the interests of Western materialism.
> — helplessly watch their diseased children suffer.
> — are trapped in a dead-end ghetto lifestyle.
> — will perpetuate child abuse through another generation of poverty.
> — will be born as drug addicts.
> — sleep on couches in other people's homes.
> — are born into large families living in a single-room homes in slum hotels.

Listen as James describes the repentance we need:

Come near to God and he will come near to you. Wash you hands, you sinners, and purify your hearts, you

double-minded. Grieve, mourn and wail. Change your
laughter to mourning and your joy to gloom. Humble
yourselves before the Lord, and he will lift you up.
(James 4:7-10)

I want to suggest that you begin your response by let-
ting your heart break. Let the tears flow as you consider
the desperate condition of people around the world. Most
of us have not been doing much for the suffering of this
world. So covenant with God, right now, by declaring you
are no longer going to hide from reality.

Too many of us have received the gospel in this
manner:

God became a man, born of the Virgin Mary. He lived
His life helping people in desperate need and ultimately died on a cross accepting upon Himself the sins
of the world. After three days God raised Him from
the dead and highly exalted Him, giving Him the
name above every name, signifying that He is the
authority figure of the universe. Someday He will
return and complete the will of God on planet earth.
He did all this in such a way that we can be His followers without really obeying Him.

Read this out loud and you'll realize how foolish it
sounds. We simply have not obeyed the King of the Universe in regard to meeting the needs of the poor. It is time
for us to get on our face before God and repent with bitter
tears.

A periodic time of fasting and praying is a second
step. Perhaps you could fast one day a week, or one weekend a month. It would be helpful to take the money you

will save and give it either to a poor person, or to someone who helps the poor. As you fast in a systematic way, ask God to show you what He wants *you* to do.

I minister at Imperial Christian Fellowship in La Mirada, California. Years ago the members there instituted the practice of a weekend fast. At the end of these weekends they gathered to pray, seeking God's will for the church. As people participated in this, an awareness of the need to help poor people grew in their hearts. They began to put legs to their understanding of God's will.

One woman was strongly led, while washing dishes one day, to telephone me at the mission. I was in at the time (miraculously, some would say) and she invited me to speak at their Sunday morning worship service. I went, not to give a sermon on helping the poor, but because God, through their fasting and praying, had led them to help the poor. I wanted to establish a relationship between them and Union Rescue Mission so skid row poor of Los Angeles could be helped through this fellowship. Since then their church has entered into a strong and dynamic ministry in cooperation with the mission.

Lifestyle — Not Suicide

As you fast and pray and give, I suggest that you begin to work on your point of view. I'm less concerned with performance than with perspective. A few years ago there was a lot of talk about lifestyle evangelism, in which sharing faith in Christ becomes characteristic of a Christian's everyday walk. My desire is for God's people to learn to be lifestyle providers. We need to make providing for the needy characteristic of our everyday walk.

Some overweight people go on a crash diet when they

set out to lose pounds. But the people who take weight off and keep it off are not those who run out and lose it all at once. They are those who make fundamental changes in their point of view about food, as well as changing their eating habits, resulting in a *lifetime* of proper nutrition. I am not looking for one grand suicidal effort. I am looking for a consistent and growing commitment on your part to be among those who are providing for the needs of the poor in the world.

Jerelyn and I have discovered a strong link in the chain binding us to the love of money: debt. We don't feel it's possible to adequately obey the demands of God toward the poor while maintaining a high debt structure. As my income has increased, our debts have piled up also, so we have as little money to give away as we have ever had, though I am making more money than I did when the children were small. We have decided to get out of debt.

I know other people whose psyches are being destroyed because they are locked by their debts into high-pressure jobs. God was serious when He command-ed us to owe no one anything except love. Our tendency to live beyond our means is one of the factors inhibiting us from being obedient, lifestyle providers to the poor of the world. I am aware that in some situations God would lead you to go into debt, but living in debt as a lifestyle is enslaving.

Our family's goal is to live in such a way on the money God enables us to earn that there is always some left over to give away. If we are consistently spending more money than we are making, it represents a choice to live above the level God has chosen for us. Like rebellion against the leadership of God, this overspending must be brought to an end.

I was chatting recently with friends who have also begun to work at getting out of debt. Discussing the expense of eating out at restaurants, we added up what we had spent, and discovered it was a substantial amount of money. In a moment of honesty we admitted we did not greatly enjoy eating out, and decided we would be better off to save our money and eat in restaurants only once every other month. When we did eat out we would go to a wonderful restaurant, where the experience would be very special.

True Recreation

Another area where Americans spend a great deal of money is entertainment. My hunch is that much of the entertainment we spend so many dollars on only makes us feel more anxious and uptight. Years ago I made a covenant with God. I said, "God, I know you don't mind me watching TV. I work hard and need to relax, but I want to examine my TV watching. If I'm genuinely enjoying a program, I'll continue watching it. But if I'm not enjoying it, I'm going to turn it off." Killing time by watching TV is a kind of suicide, and I told the Lord I didn't want to do that anymore.

I then began noticing that I usually needed something to eat while watching TV, because I was bored. In fact, a lot of the weight I struggle with came to me as I tried to amuse myself with food while watching a boring TV program. On that basis I dramatically reduced the amount of television I watched.

What about some of the other expensive entertainment options? My philosophy now is that true recreation is valuable and proper. I believe God enjoys seeing us refreshed. But much of the entertainment I've spent money on has not refreshed me. In fact, it has added to my problems.

Buying a Car

Another issue is the price of an automobile. I wonder how many *new* cars we would buy if we forced ourselves to save up money and pay the entire cost with cash? Suppose I began saving money at the rate of three hundred dollars a month. It would be a major sacrifice to put that money aside and not spend it on anything else, but in about four years I would have fifteen thousand dollars saved up.

After all that work of saving up three hundred dollars a month, every month for four years, would I be willing to pull that money out of my savings account and hand all of it over to a car dealer for the dubious privilege of driving away with a new car? No, I would more likely choose to spend three or four thousand dollars to repair the car I have.

We use the psychological denial mechanism when we put out of our minds the total price tag for a new car, and think of its cost only in terms of the monthly payment. We often fail to recognize that paying high interest represents an extremely expensive commitment.

Awake and Arise

In summary, I am suggesting that we:

— examine our lifestyle;
— covenant to develop a provider lifestyle;

— submit our spending practices to the Holy Spirit;
— and learn to spend our money joyfully and with
    real wisdom.

I don't want people to rush out and commit emotional
suicide over the issue of money. I've seen that happen
again and again. People get stirred up by the Word of God
and rush out in an unwise way. In three months time they
not only are burned out, but they are also bitter and are
spreading their bitterness to everyone they meet. Don't set
unrealistic goals. Instead, create a lifetime habit of wise
spending.

I like going to a gym and working out with exercise
bikes, weights and other aerobic equipment. Every once in
a while I'll look at all the young bucks in there with
bulging muscles and decide I want that, too. I start upping
the weight levels on the equipment I use. Soon I've
injured myself, and I'm burned out and completely off my
exercise program. But if my goal is consistency, I'm able to
keep exercising successfully.

If we are to remain consistent we'll need the help of
other people. We must be accountable to someone as we
seek to live according to God's will. In your church there
may be a number of people being stirred by God to help
the poor. You can form an accountability group to help
each other reach out to the poor, doing at least one thing
every day.

If you are alone in this endeavor, an effective aide is to
keep a journal of those you have helped. Then if you look
at your journal and see you haven't done anything for
anyone for five or six days, you can hold yourself accountable.

We need to walk in the Spirit. We need meaningful

ways to obey God, ways that are within our means, within our reach. George MacDonald gave some very practical advice:

> But I do not know how to awake and arise!
>
> I will tell you. Get up, and do something the Master tells you; so make yourself his disciple at once. Instead of asking yourself whether you believe or not, ask yourself whether you have this day done one thing because he said, 'Do it,' or once abstained because he said, 'Do not do it.' It is simply absurd to say you believe, or even want to believe in him, if you do not do anything he tells you.
>
> But you can begin at once to "be" a disciple of the Living One — by obeying him in the first thing you can think of in which you are not obeying him. We must learn to obey him in everything, and so must begin somewhere. Let it be at once, and in the very next thing that lies at the door of our conscience! (From *Creation in Christ*)

TO EASE THE PAIN IN THE HEART OF GOD

I ONCE ASKED a historian, "What would have happened in American history if American Christians in the 1840s — out of love for Christ and in response to New Testament teaching — had freed the slaves and integrated blacks into the mainstream of American cultural, economic, spiritual and emotional life? Would it have made a difference?"

Part of his answer was fairly predictable: "It would have prevented the Civil War and the decades of reconstruction, some of the most painful years in American history." Then he added, "And there is a very real possibility it would have prevented the First World War, maybe even the Second." According to this historian, the power of such a deep level of repentance would have been staggering, changing the course of the history of this nation and the world.

What would happen if American Christians in our generation simply refused to allow people to be homeless? What would happen if Christians seized our national problem of homelessness as an opportunity to express their commitment to Christ and the love of God to the world? I believe, once again, it would make a dramatic change in the course of our nation.

Dark and Unsalted

I once gave an address at the International School of Theology, associated with Campus Crusade for Christ and located near San Bernadino, California. I told the students, "Suppose the Christians in San Bernadino repented of materialism. Let's say they went into the community and saw to it that there were no widows with unpainted houses, no one sleeping in the streets, and no hungry children in the whole city of San Bernadino. After their hard work, suppose you people took your Four Spiritual Laws door to door. What difference would it make?"

The whole crowd of theology students seemed to throw themselves back in their chairs and look off in the distance, with a powerful longing for something as wonderful as that to be true. Christian love prepares the world for salvation. Jesus knew and lived that truth. He said, "You are the salt of the earth...You are the light of the world" (Matthew 5:13-14).

Because of the failure of Christians to act out what is clearly taught in the gospel, our evangelists face the difficulty of trying to win an essentially dark and unsalted society. Evangelists have to resort to techniques with which they aren't comfortable, such as taking surveys. If the world was salted and enlightened by the behavior of Christians the lost could be won effectively.

At Union Rescue Mission we used to have a church service and then offer a meal to those who attended. I began to examine this practice prayerfully and scripturally. During a study in the book of Acts, I noticed that all the witnessing opportunities sprang from two situations: First, the apostles went to synagogues and other places like Mars Hill, where people were interested in dialogue about religion and philosophy. Second, opportunities to share their faith sprang out of the dynamism of the apostles' walk with Christ. Going door to door passing out tracts was unnecessary. The apostles were constantly confronted with people willing to hear about Jesus Christ. It was not so much that the apostles went to the crowds; the crowds came to them.

So we ended the mission's practice of requiring attendance at a service before meals. We decided to try making our witness irresistible by our love and the quality of our chapel services.

I don't want to criticize people who pass out tracts or take surveys as a door-opener to witness. I respect their commitment to win the lost for Christ. Evangelism is far too basic an obligation for us ever to ignore. But what a pleasure it would be for the evangelist to work in a community well salted by brothers and sisters exercising gifts of mercy toward the poor and needy, making acceptance of the gospel natural and inevitable.

Blank Checks

If I obey God by loving the poor it will affect my prayer life as well. Nehemiah, one of my favorite Old Testament characters, was the wine server to King Artaxerxes. One day when Nehemiah served the wine, the king noticed he was sad. The king asked, "Why does your face look so sad when you are not ill?" (Nehemiah 2:2).

Nehemiah responded, "May the king live forever! Why should my face not look sad when the city where my fathers are buried lies in ruins, and its gates have been destroyed by fire?" (Nehemiah 2:3).

The king, moved by the Spirit of God, asked, "What is it you want?"

Nehemiah answered,

> "If it pleases the king and if your servant has found favor in his sight, let him send me to the city of Judah where my fathers are buried so I can rebuild it…If it pleases the king, may I have letters to the governors of Trans-Euphrates, so that they will provide me safe conduct until I arrive in Judah? May I have a letter to Asaph, keeper of the king's forest, so he will give me timber to make beams for the gates of the citadel by the temple and for the city wall and for the residence I will occupy?" (Nehemiah 2:7-8)

So Nehemiah traveled safely to Judah to rebuild the wall in Jerusalem. He carried with him a letter that, in effect, was a blank check — the king's instructions to the keeper of the forest to give Nehemiah all the lumber he wanted.

Now suppose Nehemiah had a change of mind and decided to continue on to the Mediterranean and build himself a seaside chateau, instead of going to Jerusalem? Would his guarantee of safe passage still apply if he was no longer going where the king had sent him? Would the blank check to the keeper of the forest be good if he was not doing the task the king had sent him to do? No — if he no longer was doing the task the king had assigned to him, the king's blanket promises would be of no effect.

Another fellow named Jonah was called of God to go to Nineveh and preach repentance. Instead, because he did not want to be obedient to the will of God, he ran away. He headed for Tarshish and ended up being thrown off a boat, finding himself in the belly of a great fish.

Was God obligated to answer Jonah's prayer from the belly of the fish? If it was a prayer of repentance, yes; otherwise, no. Jonah did repent, and God was with him.

Jesus has given us "blank check" promises. Here's a blank check if I've ever heard one: "And I will do whatever you ask in my name, so that the Son may bring glory to the Father. You may ask me for anything in my name and I will do it" (John 14:13-14).

Jesus grants to His disciples the use of His name. I have given my wife Jerelyn and my four daughters the use of my name. But the level to which they make use of it is limited by their maturity. My wife has absolute use of the name Caywood. She carries credit cards bearing that name and is free to sign checks, using my name as freely as I do. She and I agreed to these purposes. My children were also given my name, and if you opposed them you opposed me. I was there for them, and protected them. But I didn't give them my credit cards or allow them to sign checks.

Christians are in the same position with God. When we show our maturity, when we exercise obedience to God and begin doing the job God has given us to do, we'll find a new and exciting dynamic in using God's blank checks.

On the Offensive

We read about the ministries of ordinary men — such as George Mueller and the orphanages he founded, David Wilkerson's great work in New York City with Teen Challenge, Hudson Taylor's missionary experiences, or the establishment of Youth with a Mission by Loren Cunningham. We are stirred by the way God interacted with these people and we begin to pray and desire God's interaction with us. We are hungry for a dynamic encounter with the Spirit of God. If, when we pray, we don't get the kind of results Mueller or Wilkerson did, but only paltry and weak answers — if we become confused and doubt the promises of God — we must ask ourselves if we are walking in obedience to His will.

What is His will?

Jesus sent His disciples out into the world to destroy the works of Satan and to meet the needs of the poor. He said to Peter, "I will build my church and the gates of Hades will not overcome it" (Matthew 16:18). He is not describing a fortress church but a warlike church. He did not say, *Satan will be unsuccessful in attacking your fortress.* He said, *You will be successful in attacking Satan's fortress.*

We are to be on the offensive. It is the common experience of saints throughout history that when they go to war, God fights side by side with them. I am not sure the New Testament's blank-check promises in regard to answered prayer apply equally to Christians who want to stay within the walls of their fortresses.

A number of years ago, I was asked to minister at a wonderful church of about three hundred members. Several minutes before the service I sensed in my spirit that I had prepared the wrong message. I began asking the Lord what He wanted me to say, and I felt clearly instructed to give my personal testimony.

To be truthful, I don't like to give my testimony because it involves my failures. My wife was with me that morning and I knew my testimony is painful to her. Also I've found that most Christians believe God can set someone free from alcoholism, but not from other compulsive behavior patterns such as those in my past. As I've shared my testimony, I've at times watched people become uneasy, as if wanting to distance themselves from me. Seeing this kind of response hurts, so I don't enjoy giving my testimony.

About ten seconds before I was to stand up and preach, I still questioned this urging of the Holy Spirit. *It can't possibly be the Lord,* I rationalized. Then my wife elbowed me and said, "George, are you sure you've prepared the right sermon?" I knew I was had. It was a question of raw obedience: I could give the message I had prepared, or do what God wanted. I decided quickly to do as the Lord was directing me. Without another thought, I stood up and gave my testimony to the congregation.

I've never been comfortable standing at the back door after speaking at church services, shaking hands and listening to people say nice things about the sermon. But that morning I did want to be available, in case someone wanted to talk to me. When the service ended I stepped off the platform, and stood in front waiting to talk to whomever came forward.

A few well-wishers came by and thanked me for the message. When they had gone, I heard a man's voice from the shadows off to the right, "George, can I talk to you?"

"Sure," I said.

"I don't mean here." the man said. "In the back room. There's a little room in the back."

I said, "Okay." I walked back and met a young man who told me he was a youth leader in the church and was about to get married. But he said his life was being consumed by pornography, and he didn't know what to do about it.

I told him, "You're not going to be able to deal with this

yourself. You have to have help. I know your pastor — he's a wonderful man. Go to him and share this with him."

"Oh, no George," he said. "I'd get kicked out of the church, and that means my girlfriend…I just can't."

For the next five or ten minutes I tried to give him some hope and point him in the right direction.

When our time together ended, I was concerned because my wife didn't know where I was. As I walked back to the platform, another voice reached me from the shadows: "Can I talk to you?" So, I went back to the same room and heard the same story with different details.

This happened repeatedly for at least an hour, and I listened to man after man. I had made myself vulnerable to them, and now they were willing to make themselves vulnerable to me.

Now I was really concerned about my wife. I knew she had no idea where I was. All the while I had been trying to minister to these people I had sensed the pressure of needing to locate her.

Finally I went back into the sanctuary and started down the main aisle. The two swinging doors at the back burst open, and my wife came running through, saying, "Oh, George, I'm so sorry. I know you must have been worried, but I've been talking to the women."

Then I knew we had been set up by the Holy Spirit! He wanted us to see the heartbreak and failure among His people.

A Woman Made Beautiful

If the local church would open its doors to the broken and wounded people in this world, and if individual Christians were more willing to cash some of the blank-check promises the Lord has given us, we would learn to deal with each other's pain, too. The broken walls of Zion could be rebuilt — and that sounds a great deal like revival to me.

I am reminded of a vision I had years ago. In this vision I was in a marble-covered hotel lobby in Philadelphia (probably because Philadelphia is the city of "brotherly love"). On the other side of the lobby was a woman sitting in a wheelchair with a few people gathered around her. She was a huge, fat woman. She was poorly groomed, wore an ugly, dirty dress, and her hair was greasy and stringy. Out of her mouth rolled bitterness and anger, affecting everyone within hearing range.

I walked over behind her wheelchair, put my hands on her head and prayed for her. As I prayed, she rose up out of the wheelchair and became a lovely, well groomed, gracious woman who emanated love and compassion. I understood this was an image of the healing and restoration of the church under the anointing of Jesus Christ.

Many years ago, when the time came for me to seek a wife, I wanted a beautiful girl. God gave me Jerelyn, who is indeed a beautiful woman. I don't think Jesus is any different from me in this desire. I think He would like to have a beautiful bride.

We're told in 1 John 3:2, "But we know that when he appears we shall be like him. For we shall see him as he is." When we actually see the incredible power and beauty of our Lord Jesus Christ at His second coming, we will involuntarily become like Him. But wouldn't it be nice if, as a wedding present, those of us who love Him would fully prepare and adorn ourselves for His coming?

Are we willing to commit ourselves to battle in this world? Are we willing to give ourselves so totally to pre-

senting God's love to a needy world that we become wet
and sweaty and poor — and yet find our own hearts
transformed? Are we willing to open our lives and our
churches to the revealing light of God, accepting the process of healing until we become the beautiful and radiant
bride our Lord has a right to expect?

Sometimes I weep with longing for the church to
become the beautiful bride Jesus is worthy of. When I
glimpse what could happen in the world if we allow ourselves to fully surrender to His mercy, I'm overwhelmed
with the desire to be obedient to His Spirit and to repent
with tears of sorrow.

When tragedy strikes a family member here at the mission, or tragedy strikes a child who is part of our ministry,
my heart is broken. Once in a while a little piece of the
suffering will receive focus in the media and there will be
an outpouring of generosity toward that person. A few
months ago, for example, a paraplegic veteran was robbed
here on the street and lost his electric wheelchair. The
media picked up the story and Union Rescue Mission
could have started a wheelchair business with the number
of wheelchairs offered from people whose hearts were
touched by the story.

But the heart of God is wounded to a much greater
degree by the suffering in our country and the world. Let
us ask God to help us see it all as He does, so that — if for
no other reasons than to ease the pain in the great heart of
God, and to present His Son with a beautiful bride — it
becomes impossible for us to cease our attempt to ease
this suffering.